Kant's Concept of the Sublime
A Pathway to the Numinous

Utkal Studies in Philosophy

General Editor
Tandra Patnaik

Editors
S.K. Mohanty
A.K. Mohanty, S.C. Panigrahi

Volume One
Action, Freedom and Responsibility

Volume Two
God, Time and Evil

Volume Three
Studies on the Purusarthas

Volume Four
Reality and Mysticism

Volume Five
Social Justice: Philosophical Perspective

Volume Six
Facets of Humanism

Volume Seven
Varnadharma, Niskama Karma and Practical Morality

Volume Eight
Persons, Mind and Value

Volume Nine
Darwinism and Philosophical Analysis

Volume Ten
Kant's Concept of the Sublime

Utkal Studies in Philosophy - X

General Editor : Tandra Patnaik

Kant's Concept of the Sublime

A Pathway to the Numinous

Pabitrakumar Roy

Decent Books
New Delhi -110059

in association with

Department of Special Assistance in Philosophy
Utkal University, Bhubaneswar

Cataloging in Publication Data — DK
[Courtesy: D.K. Agencies (P) Ltd. <docinfo@dkagencies.com>]

Roy, Pabitrakumar, 1936 -
Kant's concept of the sublime : a pathway to the numinous / Pabitrakumar Roy.
110 p. 23 cm.
Includes index.
ISBN 8186921303

1. Kant, Immanuel. 1724 – 1804. 2. Sublime, The 3. Philosophy. 4. Metaphysics. I. Title.

DDC 111.85 21

ISBN 81-86921-30-3
First Published in India in 2005

Published by:
Decent Books
D-36/A-1, Mohan Garden, Najafgarh Road
New Delhi - 110 059
Ph. (011) 2535-3435

in Association with
Department of Special Assistance in Philosophy
Utkal University, Bhubaneswar

Distributed by:
D.K. Printworld (P) Ltd.
Regd. office : *'Sri Kunj,'* F-52, Bali Nagar, New Delhi - 110 015
Phones : (011) 2545-3975, 2546-6019; *Fax* : (011) 2546-5926
E-mail : dkprintworld@vsnl.net *Web* : www.dkprintworld.com

Printed by : Decent Books, New Delhi.

To

Professor D.P. Chattopadhyaya

Philosopher and Kalyānmitra

In grateful admiration

"It is much easier to point out the faults and errors in the work of a great mind than to give a distinct and full exposition of it's value."

— Schopenhauer
Criticism of the Kantian Philosophy

Contents

Foreword

A PRESSING problem that is faced by the philosophers in metaphysics and morals is the tension between the subjective and the objective points of view. How is one able to reconcile or combine a person's subjective points of view of the world with an objective view of the same world which is supposed to exist "out there," independent of our knowing of it or theorizing about it? Understanding makes nature, said Kant, but does not create her; it makes nature from out of *given* materials presented phenomenologically to the aspects of our sensitivity. The (logical) discomfiture, generally supposed to have resulted from this, is how to explain the things-in-themselves which *exist* and exist as *the cause* of the phenomena and yet are supposed not only to be unknown but also to be *unknowable*. The peculiarities of a knower's perspectives inevitably affect our knowledge of the world, which includes ourselves who are in it, and yet we crave to have an objective view of the world independent of all these personal peculiarities. We crave for objectivity which we know is not gettable. For, however hard we may try to step back and observe outside ourselves, "something will stay behind the lens, something in us will determine the resulting picture." This is how the problem presents itself to Thomas Nagel (see *The View From Nowhere*, Oxford University Press, New York, 1986, p. 68).

This is a predicament of principle, a predicament that is more endemic in matters of morality and moral valuing. For on the one hand, moral principles and moral values are stubbornly claimed to be objective and universal while, on the other, morals are intrinsically related to the will. For Kant, an act to be moral must be based on the will of the person and also (based) on a maxim that could stand as a law for all rational beings. The latter, firmly rooted in the maxim of categorical imperative and universality of morality, ingrained in the spirit of the first *Critique* of Kant, was none the less thought to be inadequate in explaining morals in their fullest implications. Kant was, therefore, dissatisfied and eager to offer a complete explanation of morality beyond the limitations of the first *Critique*, and the second.

In this brief but effective work, Professor Pabitrakumar Roy presents the Kantian answers to the problems of morals as outlined above. For a convenient starter, we may take Roy's claim that one has to go "beyond the first *Critique* of Kant focused on the methodology of the physical series and the second *Critique* focused on ethics to the third, that of aesthetic judgements" in order to find a solution to the tension between the subjective and the objective points of view and to suggest answers to the resulting problems. The aesthetic experience of the sublime fills the gap between the objectively convceived moral principle and the (subjective) motivation for moral behaviour and purportedly serves to solve the problem of the objectively conceived moral law motivating the subjective will, which Kant seems to have encountered again and again. I find a perfect parallel between this and Nagel's way of seeing the problem, though their solutions go in different ways, Nagel recommending a secondary sort of objectivity that he calls "objective tolerance" for morals as a solution to the problem at issue (see my forthcoming *Ethics and Society*, Ch. 3), though I think Kant would not strictly agree. Morality, Roy points out, provides a further dimension of completeness to our view of the self and the world towards which the theoretical reasons strive but cannot demonstrate. Kant, therefore, considers morality as an extension of theoretical reason. However, exposing the limitation of theoretical reason is not, as might be taken to be, a refutation of metaphysics on Kant's part, but rather *legitimization* of it. What, then, is the role of metaphysics in tying together aesthetics and ethics? The answer is that it is the experience of the sublime that connects aesthetics to the metaphysics of morals. Kant is seen to be continuously working towards this moral role of the sublime: while his second *Critique* argues that through pure practical reason the moral, which is the supersensible, is given objective reality — this is where clearly comes out Kant's preference for the moral sense theory, characteristic of Hutcheson, Hume and Rousseau — the third *Critique* argues that the aesthetic experience of the sublime makes the mind *feel* its moral vocation. By mind's "moral vocation" Kant meant morality to be *innate* to human nature. As Kant has implied in his third *Critique*, the supersensible is the unique meeting point of logic and metaphysics, which links together the domains of theoretical reason and moral motivation. In the introduction to the *Critique of Judgement*, we see Kant unraveling an analogous role of taste in that it serves to bridge the gulf between nature and freedom (which, for Kant, is the essence of morality). Logically taste may be independent of morality, but metaphysically it serves morality. The judgement of taste, in connection with the experience of the beautiful, provides us with a smooth transition from the sensible (knowledge of the beautiful) to the supersensible (realm of the morally good). The sublime, Roy points out, is a like state of mind as the beautiful with a similar role. The aesthetic feeling of the sublime as an experience of the supersensible has, thus, a very significant role in dealing with the problem of moral motivation. Roy has reason to claim that the experience of the sublime is not a mere pointer to our supersensible faculty, but a phenomenon that rests on metaphysical principles, for that is what Kant's aesthetics is supposed to be. We could say that for Kant, aesthetics supervenes on metaphysics and makes the latter complete and comprehensive. This is particularly true of his metaphysics of morals.

I have argued elsewhere (in my *Ethics and Society*, forthcoming, Ch.2) that man is naturally moral in the sense that he has a natural propensity to act morally and that it follows from man's being both rational as well as spiritual. While rationality makes man tell the moral from the immoral, it is the spiritual urge that makes him *identify* with the moral and motivate him towards moral behaviour and moral action. With adequate textual expertise and ease of interpretation, Roy brings out the Kantian "life long concern" with the problem of moral motivation and hence his emphasis on the feeling of the sublime. The analogue of the sublime is the spiritual urge, which I claim to be *dispositionally* constitutive of human nature. Human beings have an innate moral sense, Kant seems very much to have held, which, when nourished, motivates them towards moral behaviour and moral action. But it seems to be the paradox of the human situation that moral laws are objectively necessitating but moral motivation, strictly speaking, is not, which presumably is in the danger of being (mis)guided by inclinations. But Kant's solution to this problem, Roy points out, lies in the aesthetic judgement. It has been rightly said that it is the business of the objective will "to transcend and correct" inclinations in favour of the real — i.e., the most objectively recognizable — reasons in ethics, just as it is the business of the objective mind to "transcend and correct" appearances in favour of what there really is. (Jonathan Dancy, *Moral Reasons*, Blackwell, Oxford, 1993, p.147). The aesthetic experience of the sublime is the source of this "transcending" power of moral motivation which makes it free from the inclinations. "If morality were not independent of all inclinations," says Roy, "there could be no agreement among human beings in regard to morality," apparently pleading for the objective status of moral values. The essence of morality is that, he continues to assert, "our actions have their motivating ground in the universal rule." This theory, articulated in Kant's *Lectures on Metaphysics,* well anticipates the basic principle of his categorical imperative. But the problem, still engaging Kant, is: can the universal rule motivate the will? How, in particular, the rule of the understanding, objectively conceived, can (subjectively) motivate people to action? From the Kantian point of view, Roy finds the answer as follows:

> The understanding provides the moral judgement, but the capacity to be moved by a moral judgement is the moral feeling.

The analogue of the understanding and the moral feeling is what I claim to be man's rationality and spirituality. This moral feeling, which Kant speaks of as the "supersensible intuition," is not a theoretical requirement of our cognitive power, says Roy, but "an expansion of the mind" (*chitta vistara* — he quotes from Sri Aurobindo). Its aim is the moral, and this is the moral role of the aesthetic experience of the sublime.

In this experience, in this moral consciousness, is manifested the ultimate authority and transcendence of man's rational over his sensible being. The moral consciousness arises from his self-transcendence towards the universal. The sublime, thus, is the domain where the subjective/objective tension dissipates and the apparent duality of the noumena and the phenomens is depleted. Through this one feels the noumena and is subjectively motivated in favour of the objectively conceived moral rule. For Kant, therefore, there are no two worlds, ontologically speaking; contrary to popular readings, *there is only one world* which, grounded noumenally, is experienced as phenomena. We know the *one real world,* which appears to our sense experience. Of course, it can be *conceived* both as it appears to us *as well as* it is in itself. To put it in the Bradlean phraseology, the two are only *distinguished but not separable* aspects of reality. Kant had only one reality in mind, which is approached from two different points of view.Through the experience of the sublime one *feels* the noumenal reality — this, Kant would insist, is *cognitive* in nature — and may be subjectively motivated in favour of the objectively conceived noumena that sensible knowledge has no access to. Accordingly, the supersensible is not the supernatural.

In what follows, Professor Roy has given an excellent account of the sublime as the source of Kant's metaphysics of the morals. I am privileged to have been asked to write this foreword, which is primarily concerned to focus on the problem of morals/moral motivation that has engaged Kant and several others in moral philosophy; this brief introduction therefore, has not paid elaborate attention to some related concepts like freedom, beauty, taste and good on which Roy has offered illuminating analysis. In course of straightening the described problem and solution thereof, this Introduction might have had a few elements of my own view on morality in general and of my reading of Kant's moral philosophy in particular. But I am sure it gives a fairly faithful account of Roy's reading of Kant on morality.

Bhubaneswar **P.K. Mohapatra**
15 June, 2004 Senior Fellow, ICPR

gratitude to Messrs Decent Books, New Delhi, for collaborating with the Department of Philosophy (DSA), Utkal University, in the publication of this book.

August 17, 2004

TANDRA PATNAIK
Professor & Coordinator
Department of Philosophy
Utkal University, Bhubaneswar

It adds to my pleasure to recall the wonderful time I had as Visiting Faculty at the Utkal University. The friends at the Department of Philosophy were kind and courteous.

I would like to thank very sincerely Professors Prafulla Mohapatra, Tandra Patnaik and Aditya Mohanty who had befriended me even beyond academic engagements. Their interest in my work has made publication of this monograph possible.

In evenings I used to sit on the terrace of the University Guest House and look at the crowns of coconut trees swaying in sea breeze, silhouetted against the far away city lights. This recollection adds another pleasure.

My wife Ratnabali, has helped me as ever with Kant's German expressions. This is acknowledged with love.

August 30, 2004 **Pabitrakumar Roy**

1

Introduction

I LOOK upon Kant as a great *acharya* of freedom. This is a confessional statement which pleases me greatly.

It is possible to decipher three notions of freedom which have emerged in the tradition of Western philosophy. First, there had been a formulation of empirical freedom, to choose what one wants. John Locke saw freedom as being able to act or not act according to one's will. From Hume to Russell freedom appears as the absence of external obstacles to the realization of our desires. Individual self-realization is understood as the accomplishment of one's good as one sees it. This reflects one's personal idiosyncrasies and temperament, which in turn reflect each person's individual character. This level of freedom is reflected in the contemporary sense of "choice." Freedom becomes another name for personal willfulness.

The second level of freedom may be termed formal freedom to choose as one ought. This is a much richer notion of freedom. This acknowledges the ability of the human being to transcend the empirical order and to envisage moral laws and ideals. For Kant freedom consists not in acting merely as one pleases but in willing as one ought, whether or not this can be enacted. Moral standards are absolute and objective, not relative to individual or group preferences. How they can remain nevertheless autonomous emerges in the evolution of Kant's Three *Critiques*.

In the *Critique of Pure Reason* Kant developed a Theory of Knowledge for the universal and necessary laws of the physical sciences. Reductionist philosophies such as positivism are happy to leave the matter there, for the necessity of the sciences gives control over one's life, while their universality extends this control to others. If Kant's categories could lend rational order to the random empirical world of facts, then positivism could achieve Descartes' goal of walking with confidence in the world.

For Kant, however, this simply will not do. Clarity which comes at the price of necessity may be acceptable and even desirable for works of nature, but it is an appaling way to envisage human life. In his ethical works Kant proceeds to identify that which is distinctive of the moral order. His analysis pushes forcefully beyond utilitarian goals, inner instincts and rational (scientific) relationships, precisely beyond the necessitated order which can be constructed in terms of his first *Critique*. None of these recognizes that which is distinctive of the human person, namely, freedom. For Kant, an act, in order to be moral, must be based upon the will of the person as autonomous, not heteronomous or subject to others or to necessary external laws.

This becomes the basic touchstone of his philosophy. His critical career remains to be recontextualized in this new light. Both the *Groundwork* and the second *Critique* are composed in terms of freedom. Even the third *Critique* is also written in order to provide a context that enables the previous two *Critiques* to be read in a way that protects human freedom. In the *Groundwork*, the whole notion of law or moral rule is recast in terms of freedom. If all must be ruled by or be under law, and yet the moral act to be free and autonomous, then my maxim must be something which as a moral agent I, and no other, give to myself. This has surprising implications, for if the moral order is to be universal, then my maxim which I dedicate to myself must be fit to be also a universal law for all persons. On this basis freedom emerges in a clearer light. It is not the self-centered whim of the circumstantial freedom or self-realization of the empiricist. Neither is it a despotic exercise of the power of the will. Finally, it is not the clever self-serving eye of Plato's rogue. Rather, as the highest reality in all creation, freedom is power that is wise and caring, open to all and bent upon the realization of the ideal of a universal realm of ends-in-themselves. It is free men living together in righteous harmony.

But it is in the third *Critique* that Kant provides the needed context for such harmony. How can the newly uncovered freedom survive when confronted with the necessity and universality of the realm of science, and its implications for technology — as understood in the *Critique of Pure Reason*? Will the scientific interpretation of external nature force freedom back into the inner realm of each person's heart where it would be reduced at best to good intentions or good feelings towards others? The answer lies in existential freedom or aesthetic harmony.

When we attempt to act in this world or to reach out to other, must all our categories be universal and hence insensitive to that which marks others as unique and personal? Must they be necessary and hence leave no room for creative freedom? Must the human spirit be reduced to the sterile content of empirical facts or to the necessitated modes of scientific laws? Kant's answer is resounding: No ! Taking as his basis the reality of freedom Kant proceeds to develop his Third *Critique* as a context within which freedom and scientific necessity could coexist, indeed in which necessity would be the support and instrument of freedom. He distinguishes the two issues as reflected in the two parts of the third *Critique*. He acknowledges that nature and all reality must be teleological. For, if there is to be room for human freedom in a cosmos in which one can make necessary laws, if science is to contribute to the exercise of human freedom, the nature too must be directed toward a goal and manifest throughout a teleology with which free human purpose can be integrated. In these terms, nature, even in its necessary and universal laws, is no longer alien to freedom, and is conceivable within human freedom. The structure of the first *Critique* will not allow one to affirm this teleological character as a metaphysical reality. Hence, Kant recognizes that we must proceed *as if* all reality is teleological precisely because of the undeniable reality of human freedom in an ordered universe.

If, however, technology in principle provides the needed space there remains the issue as to how freedom is exercised, namely, what motivates it to the necessary and universal laws of science? This is the task of the "Critique of the Aesthetic Judgement" where the imagination plays the key integrating role in enabling a free person to relate to a necessary order of nature and structures in society in a way that is neither necessitated nor necessitating.

There is something similar here to the *Critique of Pure Reason*. In both, the work of the imagination in assembling phenomena is not simply to register, but to produce the objective order. As in the first *Critique* the approach is not from a set of *a priori* principles which are clear all by themselves and are used in order to bind the multiple phenomena into a unity. On the contrary, under the unity the imagination orders and reorders the multiple phenomena until they are ready to be informed by a unifying principle whose appropriateness emerges from the reordering carried out by the productive imagination.

In the first *Critique*, the productive work was done in relation to the abstract and universal categories of the intellect and carried out under a law which dictated that phenomena must form a unity. Hence, although it was a human product, the objective order was universal and necessary and the related sciences were vaild both for all things and for all people.

In the "Critique of the Aesthetic Judgement," in contrast, the imagination in working toward an integrating unity is not confined to the necessitating structures of categories and concepts, but ranges freely over the full sweep of reality in all its dimensions to see whether relatedness and purposiveness can emerge. Hence, on standing before a work of art one might focus upon its light or form, sound or word, economic or interpersonal relations — or, indeed, upon any combination of them in a natural environment or a society, whether encountered concretely or expressed in symbols.

All these ordering and reordering by the imagination can bring about numberless unities. Unrestricted by any *a priori* categories, it can integrate necessary dialectical patterns in its own free and, therefore, creative production and scientific universals within its unique concerete harmonies.

This properly creative work of the human person in this world extends the realm of human freedom to the whole of reality. For this, harmony is appreciated not merely intellectually in terms of its relation to a concept or schema (the first *Critique*), nor morally in relation to the force of a first will (the second *Critique*), but aesthetically by the pleasure or displeasure of the free response it generates. That which manifests whether a proper and authentic ordering has or has not been achieved is not a concept but the relation of pleasure with the beautiful and sublime or the disgust at the ugly and revolting which flows from our contemplation or reflection.

One could miss the integrating character of this pleasure or displeasure and its related judgement of taste. This would be so if one looked at it ideologically as simply a repetition of past tastes in order to promote stability or reductively as a mere interior or private matter at a level of consciousness available only to an elite class or related only to an esoteric band of reality. Such would ignore the structure which Kant laid out at length in his first "Introduction" to his third *Critique*. He noted there that he conceived the *Critique* not as merely juxtaposed to the first two *Critiques* of pure and practical reason, but as integrating both in a richer whole.

This opens a rich prospect for freedom in society. It need no longer be simply the capacity of the individual to gather virtues about oneself, nor the second level of freedom to set universal laws. Beyond this, it is the capacity to integrate both of them creatively into a process of shaping one's personal and social life in a unique and beautiful manner. In society this, indeed, becomes the reality of culture. Development in the level of aestheticism solitarily enables one to take into account ever greater dimensions of reality and creativity and to imagine the shapes which are richer in purpose. There must be more to the human consciousness than had thus far been explored since Bacon smashed the idols, and Descartes put all under doubt and Locke erased all in order to begin with the mind as a blank tablet. One requires to go beyond the first *Critique* of Kant focused on the methodolgy of the physical series and the second *Critique* focused on ethics to the third, that of aesthetic judgement. The development of this new level of awareness is of the greatest moment for it opens new levels of human consciousness in ways of finding unity in multiplicity.

Therefore, we are required to reconsider Kant's relation to metaphysics. A part of the intention of the present tract is to argue that Kant's philosophy deserves to be considered not as a refutation rather a legitimatization of metaphysics. This metaphysics is primarily a moral metaphysics. On taking into account the thrust of all the three *Critiques*, Kant's thesis could be said to be implying that the feeling of the sublime permits us to experience the noumenon. This can be established by the methods of contemporary research in the history of philosophy. The history of Kant's development toward the *Critique of Judgement* is itself an elaborate study. Texts by Hutcheson, Hume, Rousseau and Burke are to be accounted for in the context of the history of Kant's sources. With Kant the sublime is no mere criterion for aesthetics or a tool of poetics. It is a subject of metaphysical inquiry. The question as to what is the role played by metaphysics in tying together aesthetics and ethics? is answered by the thesis that the sublime is the doorway connecting aesthetics and metaphysics.

There has been a continuity in Kant's thought on the sublime and its moral role. This can be traced from his early writings to his mature work. The Kantian sublime has rarely been considered in the historical context. A survey of the corpus reveals Kant's life-long concern with the problem of moral motivation, which speaks to the significance of the aesthetic experience, particularly the experience of the sublime, in terms of his overall concern with morality. It is possible to consider the sublime in the context of moral motivation. Kant has argued in the second *Critique* that one may be apodictically certain that the super-sensible exists through the principles of pure practical reason, and none the less be aware that there remains a gap between the objectively conceived principle and subjective motivation. The aesthetic experience of the sublime provides an experience that helps fill this gap. Kant's mature theory of the sublime is first formulated in the *Groundwork* and then in the second *Critique*, the term "sublime" is of course used adjectivally in these works. The feeling of the sublime figures as an aesthetic experience in the third *Critique*. But whatever that may be, it is clear that Kant intends to develop a link between the sublime and morality, a connection with our self-transcendent moral consciousness and the feeling of respect. The sublime is ultimately for Kant a doorway to the super-sensible that is morally significant in that it helps to solve the problem of motivating the subject towards an objectively conceived goal. Morality gives a further dimension of completeness to our view of self and the world which theoretical reason strives towards but cannot itself demonstrate. Kant then sees morality as extending theoretical reason. In the second *Critique* it is argued that through pure practical reason the super-sensible is given objective reality, and going further in the third *Critique* Kant argues that the aesthetic experience of the sublime allows the mind to *feel* its super-sensible vocation. The Introduction to the third *Critique* makes taste serve to bridge the gulf between nature and freedom. From the *logical* point of view taste is independent of morality, but from the *metaphysical* point of view taste exists to serve morality. The *priori* principle of reflective judgement is a manifestation of our super-sensible being. And so is the sublime, In the third *Critique* Kant uses the term "super-sensible" to refer to the unity which links the theoretical and moral domains together. It is not only that the world of art can be recovered for the Kantian sublime, but the feeling of the sublime as an experience of the super-sensible can also be shown to have an importance for the problem of moral motivation.

The *Critique of Judgement* is momentous for the ethical turn given to the cognitivity of the idea of reflective judgement, and finally the metaphysical tone emphasizing the idea of the super-sensible as the ground of both subjective freedom and natural order. The sublime is important for Kant because it illuminates metaphysics. The feeling of the sublime and the elevation and awe that attend it are the highest feeling of which man is capable. This is not disputed, but there have been critics of Kant who suggesting that the experience .has analogical or metaphorical value in providing a poetic bridge to the numeral, the feeling does not afford any privileged access to the noumenal. One cannot articulate the noumenal any more than the mystic can articulate his visions. But to say that an experience cannot be articulated does not negate the possibility of the experience. I am inclined to believe, with reasons of course, that the experience of the sublime for Kant does more than merely hint at our super-sensible faculty. Kant's aesthetics rests upon metaphysical principles. The aesthetic experience is not a second-rate phenomenon, but, rather a phenomenon of the utmost existential importance.

Taking the view that the experience of the sublime was important to Kant, that the aesthetic experience, and especially the experience of the sublime was phenomenologically important to him as he persued his life-long moral project, I would endeavour to highlight his concern for moral motivation and his thought on feeling as a motive capable of moving the individual existing person in favour of objectively conceived moral law. Once this concern is understood, the importance given by Kant to the connective between the feeling of the sublime and our awareness of our own super-sensible mode of being becomes clear.

Throughout Kant's career, he was concerned with the problem of motivating the subject towards an objectively conceived goal. Kant's description of the sublime is relevant to the problem of moral motivation. The sublime moves us, and it moves us *because* of its capacity to make us aware of our moral vocation. It is for this reason that the concept of the sublime is morally and metaphysically important to Kant.

The idea that the sublime is an experience somehow moves us back to at least as far as Longinus who wrote the work entitled *On the Sublime* that the effect of elevated language upon an audience is not persuasion but transport (*On the Sublime*: The Greek Text Edited after the Paris Manuscript with Introduction, Translation, Facsimiles and Appendices, tr. W. Rhys Roberts, Cambridge, 1899, rpt. New York, 1987). The book is the earliest attempt to define the sublime extant (although it is a criticism of an earlier treatise on the sublime by Caelcilius). Briefly speaking, the sublime is a term used in literature which refers to the product of a great and noble mind presenting its ideas in such a way that it is remarkable for its instantaneous appeal. Although the theme of the sublime can be traced back to the beginnings of philosophical aesthetics, in the eighteenth century the problem of the sublime takes on a new significance.

Edward Burke's work *Enquiry into the Original of Our Feelings of the Sublime and The Beautiful* appeared in 1757, Lessing's German translation was published in 1773. Kant eventually did read it, he mentions Burke's work in the Third *Critique.* Burke's *Inquiry* constitutes the first important systematic presentation of the sublime in terms of a new and more profound concept of aeshetic subjectivity that emerged in the eighteenth century (see Ernst Cassirer, *The Philosophy of the Enlightenment,* trans., Frilz C.A. Koelln and James P. Pettegrove, Princeton University Press, 1951). David Hume's *Of the Standard of Taste* appeared in German translation by Sulzar in 1756. Recent research indicates that Kant first read them in 1760-70. There is little doubt regarding Kant's position wherein he is aware that *rational* arguments of pure practical reason are not in themselves sufficient to *move* the human being towards embracing their moral feeling. The importance of the third *Critique* lies in its articulation of the phenomenon whereby we *feel* our moral vocation. *Feeling* our moral vocation, as any reader of Hume would know, constitutes a stronger motivation to action than merely conceiving it. And Kant was very much concerned throughout his life with the problem of motivating human beings to moral action. And herein lies the importance of the feeling of the sublime. This interpretation appears to have been overlooked for the most part in the literature until now. We must not miss Kant's awareness of the need for a human being to be *moved* so opposed to or in addition to attaining rational cognition. In his pre-critical writings, such as *Lectures on Metaphysics* (tr. and ed. Kari Ameriks and Steve Naragon. The Cambridge Edition of the Works of Kant, ed. Paul Guyer and Allen W. Wood, Cambridge, Cambridge University Press, 1997), Kant suggests that the faculty of pleasure and displeasure is the faculty of being affected by objects. If we speak of an object as beautiful or ugly or agreeable or disagreeable, we speak not of the object in itself but of how it affects us. If we take away the faculty from all rational beings and increase their faculty of cognition however much, they would cognize all objects without being *moved* by them. Everything would be the same for such a being since they would lack the faculty for being affected by objects.

All pleasure and displeasure presupposes cognition of an object either in terms of sensation or intuition or of concepts. There is no desire for or satisfaction in the unknown. But pleasure is not in the *cognition,* pleasure is a *feeling* for which cognition is the precondition. What then is feeling? It is hard to determine, Kant has the following explanation to offer. Representations can be two-fold, i.e., they may be representations of the object or of the subject. Our representations can be compared either to the objects or with the entire life of the subject. The subjective representation of the entire power of life, *gesammte Lebenskraft,* for receiving or excluding objects is the relation of satisfaction or dissatisfaction. Hence *feeling is the relation of the objects* not to the representation, but rather to the entire power of the mind, (*gesammte Kraft des Gemüths*), for either most inwardly (*innigst*) receiving them or excluding them. The receiving is the feeling of pleasure and the excluding is the feeling of displeasure, *anukula* or *pratikula vedaniya.* In other words, what harmonizes with the principle of life is pleasure, and its contrary, displeasure.

Obviously then the faculty of pleasure and displeasure is wholly distinguished from the faculty of cognition. The determination of things with respect to which we manifest pleasure and displeasure are not determinations that belong simply to the objects. They are determinations that refer to the constitution of the subject. Kant distinguishes between logical and aesthetic perfection. Logical perfection agrees with the object, aesthetic perfection occurs when the comparison of representations in cognition agrees with the entire power of life or entire power of mind of the subject. Life, we are told, is the inner principle of self-activity, Life may be promoted or hindered, and the feeling of the promotion of life is pleasure, while the feeling of the hindrance of life is displeasure. Pleasure is therefore a ground of activity and displeasure a hindrance of activity. This identification of pleasure with activity foreshadows Kant's later account of the beautiful in terms of the free play (*frises Spiel*) of imagination and understanding, and of the sublime in terms of activity of imagination in the *Critique of Judgement.*

In a passage reminiscent of Plato's account of the soul, Kant distinguishes three kinds of pleasure according to three aspects of life, which is understood as the inner principle of self-activity. He defines soul in these terms when he takes up the topic under the heading of "Rational Psychology." However, there is a three-fold pleasure. Animal pleasure, which consists in the feeling of the private senses, "human pleasure," which is feeling according to a universal voice, by means of the sensible power of judgement. It is a middle thing, cognized from sensibility through an idea; and finally "spiritual pleasure," which is cognized from pure concepts of the understanding. Kant's German word for pleasure in all the three cases is *Lust,* with varying qualifiers. We are also told that pleasure and displeasure may be either objective or subjective depending upon whether its ground agrees with a determined subject or with a universal judgement that has a universal validity and is vaild for everyone, independently of the particular conditions of the subject. Objective satisfaction is two-fold: something pleases or displeases either according to universal sensibility or according to the universal power of cognition. The former is either beautiful or ugly, the latter is either good or evil. How can a human being pass judgement according to the universal sense given that one may only consider the object according to one's private sense? The answer that may be suggested 'according to Kant's mode of thinking' would be that out of the intercourse among human beings a communal sense arises which is valid for everyone. Communal sense arises only if one comes into a community, otherwise distinction between the beautiful and the ugly is impossible. When one is pleased according to a communal and universally valid sense, one has taste.

Taste however depends on the senses, hence it belongs at the base of the faculty of pleasure and displeasure. Higher up one judges objects according to universally valid grounds of the power of cognition. This is to judge whether an object pleases or displeases from cognition of the understanding according to universally valid principles. If something is an object of intellectual satisfaction, it is good, if it is an object of intellectual dissatisfaction it is evil. We may ask, how can the good please if it does not awaken any gratification? If virtues were agreeable everyone would be virtuous. Kant's answer to the question lies in *freedom*.

Freedom is the greatest degree of activity and life, and if one feels that something agrees with the highest degree of freedom, one is pleased. This is the state of being pleased with spiritual life. This pleasure is intellectual pleasure. In this state one derives satisfaction without gratification. Such intellectual pleasure is *only in morality*. From where does morality get such pleasures? Kant's answer would be that morality is the harmony of freedom with itself. Whatever harmonizes with freedom agrees with the whole of life, whatever agrees with the whole of life pleases. But this pleasure is a reflective (*reflectirende*) pleasure. We are not gratified by it, we approve of it through reflection. Morality does not gratify, but through the exercise of virtue a human being feels his spiritual life and the highest degree of freedom.

How does that which does not gratify motivate? Kant would say that if the cognition of the understanding has a power to move the subject to the action *merely because* the action is *in itself* good, then this motivating power is an incentive which we call moral feeling. There should be moral feeling then, whereby a motive power arises through the motives of the understanding. This incentive of the mind is not pathologically necessitating, that is the principle of morality is *not* derived from the subjective grounds of our moral feeling.

Moral feeling is a problematic term for Kant. He seems to hold that human beings have an innate moral feeling which may be nourished or suppressed and which motivates them towards moral behaviour. Are we to think of such a feeling in terms of moral motivation? How can one cognize the good through the understanding and yet have a feeling of it? How can one have a feeling of that which is cognized objectively through the understanding and is thus not an object of feeling? Is there not a contradiction? If we do the good through a feeling, then the good must be agrrable. But the good cannot at all affect our senses. Yet we call the pleasure in the good a feeling because we cannot otherwise express the subjective driving power of objective practical necessitation. This is one of the paradoxes of the human situation. Moral laws are objectively necessitating, but not so subjectively. The solution to the problem Kant proposed to find in the aesthetic judgement. In the *Lectures in Metaphysics* we find the themes that gestate till they are articulated in the critical system of the third *Critique*.

If one cares to take into account another pre-critical work of Kant, namely, the *Lectures on Ethics* (tr. Louis Infield with an introduction by Lewis White Beck, London, Methuen, 1979) one would find him addressing the problem of motivation once more. The question is what moves us to live according to the moral law? This question anticipates the famous question about the interest of reason. The latter question is in the domain of the understanding, and can be answered straightforwardly once certain criteria are adopted. But the former question is more problematic. How does the understanding move the will? How can the cognitive faculty move the faculty of desire? The answer will involve the faculty of the feeling of pleasure and displeasure which connects these two faculties. This is a solution consistent with Kant's passion for architectonics (see for example, Section 1 of the first Introduction, to the *Critique of Judgement* "On Philosophy as a System"). Kant's answer involves moral feeling, and the question speaks to the problem of access to understanding. He speaks of the principle of appraisal of obligation, which is the objective ground, but *not yet the subjective ground*. The subjective motive is that which impels us to do the thing that the understanding tells us to do, and this is moral feeling. Such a principle of motive cannot be the principle of judgement, which is rooted in the under-standing. The norm is the understanding, which contains the supreme principle of morality, but the motive is moral feeling. Motive does not take the place of the norm. When judgement is lacking, we have a theoretical fault, when motive is lacking we have a practical fault.

Kant is not at all comfortable with the concept of moral feeling. In order to come out of the discomfort he distinguishes two pathological principles : physical feeling and pathological feeling. The former aims at the satisfaction of inclinations. The latter satisfies an inclination directed to morality. But is such a feeling possible? A feeling that aims at the satisfaction of an inclination directed to morality would have to be grounded in an intellectual inclination. A feeling for objects of the understanding is an absurdity. A feeling cannot be both intellectual and sensory. And even if it were possible that we should have a sensation for morality, no rules could be established on that principle. When Kant says that a moral feeling ought to happen, whether it pleases us or not, his intention is to mean that such a feeling is not satisfaction of our inclination. A feeling can have only private validity and is not accessible to anyone else. Once anyone appeals to a feeling he gives up all grounds of reason.

A moral feeling is expected to be free of all inclination except the desire to submit to a judgement of the understanding. What then is the role of the understanding in morality? The principle of prudence is a pseudo-principle, and morality cannot be grounded on it. If morality were not independent of all inclinations, there could be no agreement among human beings in regard to morality, since everyone would seek happiness according to their own inclination. The principle of prudence is mediated through inclination, but the principle of morality is immediately known through the understanding. It is thus an utterly pure intellectual principle of pure reason. Such a principle cannot be external. The ground of morality must be an inner principle, it is *intellectuale internum,* internal to the mind. It must be sought through pure reason in the action itself. In the *Lectures* Kant does not formulate the categorical imperative as we have come to know it, but he does articulate the basic principle: namely, morality is the conformity of the action to a universally valid law of free choice. All morality is the relationship of the action to the universal rule. The essential part of morality is that our actions have their motivating ground in the universal rule. But the question remains unanswered how can the universal rule motivate the will?

Kant was well aware of the difficulty in answering the question. The understanding is the faculty of rules. If our actions are consistent with the universal rule they are consistent with the understanding, and in that case our actions will have motivating grounds in the understanding. If the action is done because it concurs with the universal rule of understanding it comes from a pure principle of morality internal to the mind. Since the understanding is the faculty of rules and judgement, morality consists in the subordination of the action to the principle of the understanding. The problem lies in explaining how a rule of the understanding, conceived objectively, can motivate subjectively, i.e., become a principle of action. Kant is dissatisfied with his own explanation. He remarks that nobody can or ever will comprehend how the understanding should have a motivating power. The understanding can of course or admittedly judge, but this judgement be given power so that it becomes motivational to impel the will on performance of an action. To understand which is "the philosopher's stone" (as mentioned in the *Lectures on Ethics*) this explanation forces Kant back to the concept of moral feeling. The understanding provides the moral judgement, but the capacity to be *moved* by a moral judgement is moral feeling. How this happens, or exactly why it is not a species of inclination is not explained — it is "the philosopher's stone."

The understanding *per se* opposes everything that is contrary to rule. Immoral actions are contrary to rules since they cannot be made into a universal *law*. Does there reside a moving force in the understanding? Only a sensibility in accordance with the motive power of the understanding would be a moral feeling. The moving force of the understanding will have to motivate subjects, not all of whom demonstrate moral feeling. For a solution of the problem we have to wait till the publication of the third *Critique.* So far Kant's explanations have been tentative, nevertheless.

We may for a while look back and consider Kant's relationship with the moral sense school. Decades before the third *Critique* (1790) Kant published a work that dealt with the sublime directly, namely, *Observations on the Feeling of the Beautiful and Sublime* (1763). All through the period of 27 years he sustained the belief that the aesthetic and the moral experiences are closely related. Kant mentioned Hutcheson in an essay of 1764, and hoped that Hutcheson's work on moral feeling might throw some light on the problem of moral obligation. Later he identified Shaftesbury and Hutcheson as leading authors of the system of ethics that is grounded on a moral feeling. But what they meant by moral feeling had never been what Kant meant by the term or expression. Kant's concern with the problem of moral obligation revolved round the issue that unless the end is shown to be necessary, there can be no obligation to order one's actions to that end. Kant rejects moral feeling as the ground of morality. He inclines towards distinguishing the objective ground whereby we discriminate what is good and bad from the subjective ground which moves us to perform the action as determined by the understanding. For Kant moral feeling cannot be the objective ground, but it is the subjective motive. But it must be admitted on all courts that moral feeling is a problematic term in Kant. His use of the term is not entirely unrelated to an understanding of moral feeling in terms of an innate human quality. The potential to experience self-satisfaction exists before the actual feeling of it. There has been a conflict between aesthetic and moral values in modern thought, and Kant represents a significant stage in the breakdown of the synthesis between the two values reached by the early phase of the Enlightenment. And hence the doctrine of the second *Critique* is that moral emotion is essentially negative in character. The paradox in Kant is that he begins by inclining on the separation of duty from happiness, and seeks to end up with reuniting them in a manner which may appear gratuitous and artificial (see John Andrew Bernstein, *Shafterbury, Rousseau and Kant: An Introduction to the Conflict between Aesthetic and Moral Values in Modern Thought,* London and Toronto, Associated University Press, 1980). The remark is somewhat harsh, but none the less worth pondering over.

2

Transcendental Freedom

HUME'S empiricism denies free-will, and without free-will there is no morality or human dignity for Kant. In a piece of correspondence Kant writes:

> There is freedom in man, versus there is no freedom, only the necessity of nature — that is what first aroused me from my dogmatic slumber and drove me to the critique of reason itself, in order to resolve the scandal of ostensible contradiction of reason with itself.
>
> — *Philosophical Correspondence* 1759-99,
> ed and tr. Arnulf Zweig,
> Chicago University Press, 1967.

So it was the antinomy of reason, especially with regard to the possibility of freedom (and with that the possibility of morality as Kant understands it) that roused him from his dogmatic slumber. In the first *Critique* transcendental freedom is a spontaneous causality, free from the efficient causality of nature, a free-will. It is an idea of reason to which no object of experience can correspond. We can never infer from experience the existence of anything that cannot be thought in accordance with the laws of experience. In a famous formulation, Kant says that ideas of reason are always either too large or too small for a concept of the understanding (A 422/B 450; A 486/B 514). That is to say there can be no *knowledge* of freedom. Further, reason does not really generate concepts, the most it can do is free a concept of the understanding from the unavoidable limitations of a possible experience (A 408/B 435). The Transcendental Analytic has established that there are no exceptions in the sensible world to the efficient causality of nature (A 536/B 564). What then of morality? A dialectic of reason has arisen, and unless it is solved we have to give in to either Hume's empiricism or metaphysical dogmatism. In either case there is no morality for Kant.

The issue is unavoidable on the part of speculative philosophy, but it must clear the way for morality. The solution is sought by proposing the point of view called transcendental idealism. Accordingly, appearances are not things in themselves, and do not exist outside the mind (A 492/B 520). But do they have an intelligible cause, which is reality, beyond the conditions of space and time? If we hold that appearances are things in themselves, there is no freedom, nature will be the complete and determining cause of every event. If, on the other hand, appearances are not taken to be more than they are, if there are only representations, they must have a ground that is not appearance, i.e., an intelligible ground. The *effects* of such an intelligible cause *appears* and are then subject to the laws of appearances and can be determined through other appearances, but the *causality* of this intelligible cause is not so determinable (A 536/B 564). This is the definition of freedom. Neither the possibility nor the existence of transcendental freedom is demonstrable. The best we can do is to show that causality through freedom is at least not *incompatible* with the efficient causality of nature (A 558/B 586). But this is not nothing, Kant's argument at least clears the way for morality.

Much has been written about the consistency of this solution. One might suggest that Kant's formal, *a priori* conditions of human experience should be thought of as epistemic as opposed to ontological. In a revealing passage in the third *Critique* Kant says it is the antinomous character of reason that forces reason to regard things in the world as appearances based on a supersensible substrate. Otherwise reason could not bring itself to accept such a principle which greatly narrows the area in which it can speculate. There have been critics also who deny that the phenomenon/noumenon distinction carries with it any ontological or metaphysical theory involving two different worlds, one more real than the other (see Henry Allison's *Kant's Transcendental Idealism: An Interpretation and Defense,* Yale University Press, 1983 for a philosophical defense, and Christine M. Korsgaard's *Creating the Kingdom of Ends,* Cambridge University Press, 1996 for a denial). I, for one, feel inclined to take noumenon and phenomenon as two ways of looking at one reality.

Freedom, then, and morality are ideas of reason, and these ideas cannot be known since they cannot be contained under a concept of understanding. Yet one can hardly deny that at its most fundamental level. Critical philosophy is a transcendental defense of a conception of reason as the supreme end-determining power. It is owing to this fact that transcendental freedom is of paramount importance to Kant's moral philosophy. Though officially speaking, freedom cannot be known, yet it is hardly deniable that there are passages in the first *Critique* that seem to indicate there is real knowledge of the noumenal self not only practically (as the faculty of reason) but also cognitively (as the faculty of the understanding). The passages numbered A 546-47/B574-75 are crucially relevant in this regard. It is true that freedom cannot be demonstrated, yet Kant does seem to want to say there are other doorways to freedom and experience of the super-sensible. If such an experience exists, it would solve the problem of moral motivation. To have been able to do that would be getting hold of the "philosopher's stone."

The problem of an objectively conceived moral law motivating the subjective will is addressed again in the second

Critique. Only the moral law, which is a product of pure practical reason can *determine* the will. But as Kant develops his position in the Analytic, we are told that frequent practice in conformity with the objectively determined moral law can produce subjectively a feeling of satisfaction with oneself. Kant calls this feeling of self-satisfaction that results from conforming to the moral law as "moral feeling" (*moralische Gefühl).* We have a duty to establish and cultivate this moral feeling, although the concept of duty is *not* derived from this feeling of self-satisfaction (see Remark II on Theorem IV Section 8 of the Analytic of Practical Reason). I would like to quote the passage which it so richly deserves:

> I am far from denying that frequent practice in accordance with this determining [as the human will by virtue of its freedom is directly determined by the moral law] can itself finally cause a subjective feeling of satisfaction. Indeed, it is a duty to establish and cultivate this feeling, which alone deserves to be called the moral feeling.

Besides, Kant talks about incentives as the subjective determining ground of the will of a being where reason does not *by its nature* necessarily conform with the objective law. Even though Kant remains true to his position that only if the principles of morally valid law are derived *a priori* it can carry with it absolute necessity, yet he acknowledges that experience shows that human beings are not always persuaded by reason, especially when reason opposes desire. Hence, in chapter III of the *Analytic of Pure Practical Reason,* entitled "The incentives of Pure Practical Reason," Kant notes in a candid manner:

> How a law in itself can be the direct determining ground of the will (which is the essence of morality) is an insoluble problem for the human reason. It is identical with the problem of how a free-will is possible. Therefore, we shall not have to show *a priori* why the moral law supplies an

> incentive but rather what it effects in the mind, so far as it is an incentive.

We need not follow Kant through his tortuous argument. But the point worth our consideration is that the moral law is the form of an intellectual causality which we call freedom. As the moral law opposes its subjective antagonists it becomes the object of respect, and in doing so it becomes the ground of a positive feeling. This feeling's origin is not empirical, since its ground is cognized *a priori*. Respect (*Achtung*) for the moral law is a feeling that is produced by an intellectual ground. It is the only feeling that we can see the necessity of end cognized *a priori*. Kant's solution to the problem of the incentives is to derive a feeling from an intellectual ground. As a feeling it is subjective and empirical and so can motivate the individual will; as derived from an intellectual ground it escapes being called pathological. The moral law is subjectively a ground of respect. It becomes possible to realize *a priori* that the moral law can exercise an effect on feeling. The effect on feeling is negative in rejecting sensible impulses opposed to the moral law, and it is positive in and through the rejection. It modifies the principle of self-love through respect for the law. The negative effect is called humiliation and is pathological. In relation to its positive ground, the moral law, the feeling of a rational subject not affected by inclinations, is called respect for the law. The feeling of respect moves resistance to the moral law out of the way. This removal of hindrance is esteemed as a positive furthering of its causality. In this positive sense, the feeling can be called a feeling of respect for the moral law while on both grounds together it can be called a moral feeling. The moral law thus has influence on the sensibility of the subject through the feeling of respect. Respect effects a feeling conducive to the influence of the moral law upon the will. Respect for the law is not the incentive to morality, it is morality itself subjectively considered as an incentive. Respect for the law is an effect on feeling, and this feeling (i.e., the moral feeling) is produced solely by reason, and serves only to make the moral law its subjective ground of action or maxim.

Respect has an effect on the feeling of pleasure and displeasure. When we compare ourselves to the moral law, we feel humiliated as the moral quality makes us aware of our own inadequacy. When self-conceit is laid aside, one can never get enough of contemplating the majesty of the moral law. Thus there is also little displeasure in it in the feeling. But since the constraint is exercised by the law of the subject's *own* reason, it contains something *elevating*. When we pursue our duty we find our soul strengthened and elevated by our realization that human nature is capable of holding itself above everything that nature can present as an incentive in opposition to it. We realize that we need not give in to inclination under any circumstances. This is strikingly similar to Kant's account of the dynamically sublime in the third *Critique,* in the experience of which we realize that we need not give up our highest principles even in the face of nature's might.

Kant defines duty as the consciousness of a free submission of the will to the moral law. This submission is a constraint on the sensibly affected subject, and the feeling of duty tends towards displeasure rather than pleasure, as does respect. The subjective effect of duty on feeling can be called self-approbation. In cognizing oneself as determined to an action solely by the moral law and without any interest, the subject becomes conscious of an altogether different interest subjectively produced by the law, which is purely practical and *free.* Kant calls this "moral interest." This feature of respect foreshadows the role assigned to the sublime in the third *Critique.* Indeed in a passage in which Kant is so overcome that he lapses in poetic: "*Duty* Sublime and mighty name . . ."

etc., This would of course recall the opening lines of Wordswoth's *Ode to Duty*.

Stern Daughter of the Voice of Good!
O Duty! If there name thou love
who art a light to guide, a rod
To check the erring, and reprove,
Then who art victory and law
When empty terrors overawe,
From vain temptations dost set free,
And calm'st the weary strife of frail humanity.

The passage illustrates again the connection between morality and the sublime in Kant. However, in the passage he tells us that duty is nothing else than what elevates a human being above himself as a part of the sensible world and connects him with an order of things that only the understanding can think. Duty is nothing other than personality, which is freedom and independence from the mechanism of the whole of nature.

It should be noted that the sublimity of the moral law is more than a metaphor for Kant. Not only does he use the language of the aesthetics of the sublime in describing the moral law, but also gives an analogous interpretation of the origins of the feelings of sublimity and respect. In both, there is humiliation of thwarting of our sensuous nature (our perceptual faculty and imagination in the sublime, our feeling of worth in respect) and also transmuted into a kind of elation by the discovery in ourselves of a power superior to that which has humiliated us (in the sublime) and superior also to that power in us which has been humiliated (in feelings of both respect and of the sublime). Respect for the law and respect for our personality are not distinct and even competing feelings, as are the two feelings which merge in our experience of the sublime. The *Critique of Practical Reason*, then yields support for the view that the sublime and the moral are closely related. We also discover that the feeling of respect and its corollary duty provide a doorway to the super-sensible world. The moral law gives freedom (and so the super-sensible) of objective reality, and that the soul believes itself elevated as we recognize the majesty of the moral law. Hence there is a *kind* of cognitive doorway to the supersensible through the moral law.

It remains to be seen that *in addition* to the doorway to the noumenon through the cognitive faculty, there is in Kant another doorway to the noumenal through the faculty of pleasure and displeasure.

In the "Introduction" to the third *Critique* Kant writes that philosophy is systematically divided according to the two possible kinds of concepts and their respective principles, namely, concepts of nature and concepts of freedom. Concepts of nature make possible a theoretical cognition governed by *a priori* principles, the concept of freedom concerns principles for the determination of the will. Accordingly theoretical or natural philosophy is epitomized in the first *Critique*, practical or moral philosophy finds explication in the second *Critique*. The third, the *Critique of Judgement* is meant to provide a bridge between the realm of nature and the realm of freedom.

The power of judgement is a mediating link between understanding and reason. The feeling of pleasure and displeasure is the mediating link between our cognitive power in general and the power of desire. Kant explains that all the powers of the mind can be reduced to the triad, namely the cognitive power, the feeling of pleasure and displeasure and the power of desire. The faculties are based in their employment on the cognitive power, although not always on *cognition*. Cognition, properly speaking, requires both an intuition and a concept (B 146 and B 51/B 75). And it is possible for the cognitive power to apprehend intuitions, pure or empirical, without concepts. When this occurs, as it does in aesthetic judgement, the presentations of the three faculties of the mind are apprehended by the cognitive power but are not cognized strictly speaking. The operation of all the three principal mental powers is based on the congnitive power even though its own intuitions and the presentations of the feeling of pleasure and displeasure and the power of desire do not suffice to yield cognition. We find that each of the three principal mental faculties are referred to corresponding higher mental powers that operate according to formal or *a priori* principles. These higher faculties are understanding, judgement and reason, and their formal principles are lawfulness, purposiveness, and obligation, (i.e., purposiveness that is also a law) respectively. The operation of these higher mental faculties according to their respective *a priori* principles yields our knowledge of nature, art and morals. The first *Critique* deals with the cognitive power, the second *Critique* deals with the power of desire, and finally, the *Critique of Judgement* deals with the feeling of pleasure and displeasure. Thus is the critical enterprise completed.

Certain points deserve our special notice: the mediating link between the cognitive power and the power of desire is a *feeling*. A feeling cannot be knowledge, but we do *experience* feeling, it is phenomenal, while transcendental freedom cannot be an object of any possible experience (recall the *third Antinomy* in the first *Critique*), we do *feel* the free play of our powers of imagination and understanding when we are in the presence of a beautiful object. We *experience* our transcendental freedom indirectly in the presence of the beautiful. The feeling of the sublime is the result of the free play of the imagination and reason. The feeling is the critical arch between the two cognitive powers.

The aesthetic experience gives us reason to believe that nature is supportive of our moral vocation. Kant holds that the causality of nature presupposes the concept of purposiveness, which is the formal principle of the faculty of judgement.

We must assume a law governed unity in nature if our empirical cognition is to form a coherent experience. The transcendental principle of the purposiveness of nature is the transcendental concept which must guide us when reflecting on objects of nature if investigation of nature is to make sense.

Purposiveness is either subjective or objective, and accordingly the *Critique of Judgement* is divided into its two parts, the "Critique of Aesthetic Judgement" and the "Critique of Teleological Judgement." Aesthetic judgement is the power to judge formal or subjective purposiveness of nature through the feeling of pleasure and displeasure. Teleological judgement is the power to judge the real or objective purposiveness of nature through understanding and reasons.

In the first "Introduction" Kant explains that in a teleological judgement, nature is regarded as purposive objectively, i.e., by reference to the possibility of the object itself. In an aesthetic judgement, nature is regarded as purposive subjectively, i.e., with reference to the subject's way of presenting something. In the case of a beautiful object, the purposiveness is attributed in the aesthetic judgement to the thing and to nature itself. But there is a different aesthetic judgement in the case of the sublime. The presentation of the sublime is applied to a purposiveness having *a priori* in the subject, namely, the super-sensible vocation of the subject's mental powers. The presentation of the sublime arouses a reflective feeling of purposiveness in the subject, which refers not to a purposiveness of nature concerning the subject, but rather to a possible purposive *use* we can make of the form of certain sensible intuitions. In aesthetic judgements regarding the sublime we make a contingent use of the presentation, not for the sake of cognizing the object as we do through the feeling associated with the beautiful, but for the sake a feeling of the inner purposiveness in the predisposition of our mental power. The "Critique of Aesthetic Judgement" is divided into a critique of taste, which is the ability to judge the beautiful, and a critique of intellectual feeling (*Geistesgefühl*), the ability to present the sublimity in objects. By the time the *Critique of Judgement* is published the "Critique of intellectual feeling" has become the "Analytic of the Sublime."

In the published "Introduction" to the third *Critique* Kant is more explicit about the arch between nature and freedom. Between the domain of nature, the sensible and the domain of freedom, the super-sensible the gulf, is immense. The sensible cannot have any influence over the super-sensible, but Kant requires for the sake of morality that the super-sensible *must* influence on the sensible. No transition from the sensible to the super-sensible through theoretical reason is possible. But the concept of freedom must be able to actualize its purpose in the world of sense. It is then possible to think of nature as being such that the lawfulness in its form will harmonize at least with the possibility of achieving the purposes of the laws of freedom in nature. Nature must in some way support the noumenal ends of freedom. The laws of causality must be somehow compatible with the laws of freedom. There must be a basis uniting the super-sensible that underlies nature and the super-sensible contained practically in the concept of freedom, even though the basis cannot be cognized theoretically or practically. The basis Kant has in mind is the basis of aesthetic judgement. It is aesthetic judgement that makes possible the transition from our way of thinking in terms of principles of nature to our way of thinking in terms of freedom.

Kant will argue that the experience of the sublime is the feeling of the inner purposiveness in the predisposition of our mental powers, namely our super-sensible moral vocation. The vocation of the human being is to be the ultimate purpose of nature and that nature's ultimate purpose must be to prepare human beings for the achievement of that ultimate purpose.

This Sāmkhya like thesis is taken up in the Section 83 of the *Critique of Judgement*. In this connection Kant makes very significant remarks about culture and civil society in which alone the fine arts and sciences can flourish. We shall have occasion later to talk about the important notions. It may suffice presently to say that a universally communicable pleasure associated with fine arts and sciences undermine the tyranny of the senses and prepares us to embrace the ends of our reason under laws of freedom. Culture strives to give us an education that makes no receptive to purposes higher than those that nature itself can provide. Kant uses culture to try to understand the relation of nature to individuals possessing the capacity for rational freedom.

The aesthetic experience, then, is for Kant, that which mediates between the relam of nature and the realm of freedom through the feeling of pleasure and displeasure. Moreover, especially through the experience of the sublime, it is a kind of doorway to the super-sensible. It gives us experiential evidence that what we do in fact exist as both phenomenal and noumenal beings, and that the transcendental ideas might be for us more than mere postulates of pure practical reason. If this interpretation is of any worth and ineluctable, then we see that the experience of the feeling of the sublime adds a more immediate level of moral motivation to the incentives of pure practical reason described in the second *Critique*.

3

Analytic of the Beautiful
The Judgement of Taste

AN AESTHETIC judgement that concerns the beautiful is a judgement of taste. In such a judgement the presentation of the object is not referred to the understanding so as to give rise to a cognition, rather, the presentation of the object is referred to by the imagination of the subject and his or her feeling of pleasure or displeasure. In fact, the presentation of a beautiful object cannot be referred to any determinate concept of the understanding. It is precisely this indeterminacy that constitutes the quality of beauty. Hence the judgement of taste is reflective. Judgement in general is the ability to think the particular as contained in the universal. If the universal is given, the judgement that subsumes the particular under it is determinative. If only the particular is given and the universal must be found, the judgement is reflective. One may suggest drawing on this definition of reflective judgement that it becomes the basis of a reflective interpretation whereby the interpretation of nature becomes hermeneutical rather than systematic.

The judgement of taste is a disinterested one. It is concerned with the mere contemplation of its object rather than its existence. Interest is the likings connected with an object's existence, and such liking refers to our power of desire rather than to our feeling of pleasure and displeasure. What the senses like in sensation is the agreeable, when we find an object agreeable, we desire objects of that kind. The liking is more than a mere judgement about the form of the object, it means that the existence of the object has been referred to our state of being insofar as that state of being is affected by the agreeable object. The agreeable object arouses in us a pleasant feeling based on our relationship to its presence. We have an *interest* in its existence, "All interest ruins a judgement of taste" says Kant. "Any taste remains barbaric if its liking requires that *charms* and *emotions* be mingled in, let alone if it makes these the standard of approval. A *pure judgement of taste* is one that is not influenced by charm or emotion (though they may be connected with a liking for the beautiful), and whose determining basis is therefore merely the purposiveness of the form" (*Critique of Judgement*, 68-9, tr. Pluhar, Hackett Publishing Company, 1987)

When we like a thing through its mere concept, by means of our reason, we call it good. If we like a thing and call it good for its own sake, it is intrinsically good. If we like it for the sake of something else it is good as a means. In both cases the concept "good" is always the concept of a purpose, i.e., either it has worth in itself as an end or it is useful as a means to some other end. The concept of purpose involves a relation of reason to at least a possible volition, and so an interest in the existence of the object of action. When we call an object good, it becomes an object of the will through principles of reason under the concept of a purpose. Both the agreeable and the good then are always connected with an interest in their object. This holds not only for goods that are means to ends but also for what is good absolutely, namely the moral good. Kant remarks that in order to consider something good we have to know what sort of the thing the object is meant to be. We must have a determinate concept of it. Beauty however needs no determinate concept. The liking for the beautiful depends on a reflection regarding the object that leads to some concept, although which one is it is indeterminate. The agreeable depends entirely on sensation and does not involve reflection, nor does it involve the concept of a purpose.

"Taste is the ability to judge an object, or a way of presenting it, by means of a liking or disliking devoid of all interest. The object of such a liking is called beautiful." This is Kant's celebrated definition of the Beautiful in the third *Critique*. The fact that we like something without any interest (which is subjective) leads us to believe that our judging contains a basis for expecting the same judgement from everyone. Since the liking does not depend on subjective conditions, we regard it as based on what we presuppose in everyone, namely the basic nature of the human mind. We tend to regard beauty as a characteristic of the object and expect others to agree with our judgement, even though the aesthetic judgement really refers to the mental state aroused in the subject by the presentation of the object. We presuppose the aesthetic judgement to be valid for everyone as if it were a judgement of logic. But this universality cannot arise from concepts since the feeling of pleasure and displeasure is not based on concepts. This claim to universality not based on concepts Kant calls "subjective universality." Kant's claim to the subjective universality of the aesthetic judgement is the focus of Paul Guyer's *Kant and the Claims of Taste*. The universality that does not rest on concepts of the object is *general validity*. This is the validity that a presentation referred to the feeling of pleasure and displeasure may have as opposed to the validity of a presentation referred to the cognitive power. Kant in fact speaks of two kinds of validity: subjective universal validity and objective universal validity. The latter is the validity of a logical judgement. It follows that as the aesthetic judgement does not rest on a concept, it does not deal with the object itself. Its validity is not a result of a connection of the predicate "beauty" and the mental realm of judging persons who encounter the object which call beautiful.

Why is this so? Why do we expect agreement when we judge an object beautiful? In judging objects in terms of concepts we demand objective or logical universal validity. Again, as and when we judge objects merely in terms of concepts we lose all presentation of beauty. There can be no rule by which we could demand the acknowledgement of another that an object is beautiful. The beautiful does not fall under a rule or the categories, when we encounter the beautiful, we want to submit the object to our own eyes *as if* our liking of it depended on the sensation. But when we say an object is beautiful we hear a "universal voice," and it is on that basis that we expect agreement from everyone. Kant says at this point "that nothing is postulated in a judgement of taste except such *universal voice* about a liking unmediated by concepts. Hence all that is postulated is the *possibility* of a judgement that is aesthetic and yet can be considered valid for everyone. The judgement of taste does not *postulate* everyone's agreement . . . , it merely *requires* this agreement from everyone, as an instance of a rule, an instance regarding which it expects confirmation not from concepts but from the agreement of others" (Pluhar, 60).

The universal voice is an idea. Where does this universal voice come from? What kind of idea is it? An idea of reason presumably. May we take it to stand for intersubjective validity? In his pre-critical lectures on Metaphysics, Kant had spoken of the universal sense that arises among human beings in community with each other. It could be that the judgement of taste depends on some such sense. The idea that the aesthetic judgement somehow involves a universal goes back at least as far as Aristotle's *Poetics*. However, we may suggest that one's judgement does in fact refer to this idea by being conscious that one's liking does not depend on the agreeable (sense of liking) or the good (liking under a concept). Only then can one count on everyone's assent, why are we justified in this claim?

The feeling of pleasure we associate with the beautiful object does not come before the judgement that the object is beautiful. Agreeableness in sensation, by its very nature, can have only private validity. The judgement that an object is beautiful does not lie in the sensation of it (the agreeable) or on its concept (the good). The judgement is the result of a state of mind. We are aware of this state through the feeling that results from the free play of the imagination and the understanding occasioned by the presentation of the object. Kant says that the mental state is communicable, and the property of communicability underlies the judgement of taste. Pleasure in the object must be the consequent of this subjective condition, not its antecedent. Still the question remains how can this mental state underlying the judgement of taste be universally communicable?

Objective communication involves cognition. The presentation, called beautiful, is subjectively determined, it does *not* involve a concept of the object. If only cognitions are communicable how can there be any basis for the universal communicability of the presentation we call beautiful? The presentation is privately determined, subjective determination of it does *not* involve a concept of the object. Yet it can be communicated because the subjectively determined basis of the presentation is nothing other than the mental state that we find in the relation between the presentational powers of imagination and understanding insofar as they refer a given presentation to *cognition in general*. The presentation of the beautiful object is referred to cognition as a universal reference point, and we can therefore expect and require the agreement of all other similarly constituted rational minds. An important precursor of the idea that the perception of beauty involves a normative judgement is St. Augustine. We can perceive the ordered object as being what it ought to be. The disordered object falls short, and so the painter can make corrections as he goes along and the critic can judge. But this rightness and wrongness cannot merely be sensed. The spectator must bring with him a concept of ideal order, given to them by a divine illumination from which it follows that judgement of beauty is objectively valid and that there can be no relativity in it in the matter. Augustine puts the question whether we have to call something beautiful because we like it or whether we like it because it is beautiful.

Now to return to Kant. The judgement that a thing is beautiful is a state of mind occasioned by the presentation of the object. When in the presence of the beautiful, the mind's cognitive powers are brought into play, as they would be when in the presence of any object, knowledge of cognition occurs when the manifold of intuition is combined by the imagination *(Einbildungskraft).* Imagination synthesizes the manifold given in pure intuition. It associates the discrete parts of the manifold with one another. Imaginations brings the manifold of intuition into the form of an image. Imagination is also the faculty that (re)presents the image of an object in its absence, (A 115, B151), under a concept given by the understanding (*Verstand*). Understanding is the faculty of *rules*. Kant defines the understanding in different ways, as a spontaneity of knowledge, as a power of thought, as a faculty of concepts and as a faculty of judgements. He says that once these definitions are adequately understood they are identical and so the understanding may be characterized as the faculty of *rules*, (A 126). In the A version of the *Transcendental Deduction*, Kant says that we ourselves introduce the order and regularity in the appearances which we call nature (A 125), and in spite of the apparent exaggeration and absurdity, the understanding is itself the source of the laws of nature and so the formal unity of nature.

The empirical laws (of nature) do not derive their origin from pure understanding. They are only special determinations of the pure laws of understanding under which, and according to the norm of which, they first become possible (A127-28).

The explicit claim that the understanding is the source of the laws of nature is abandoned in the B version, but the understanding remains the faculty of rules or principles, *a priori* of the possibility of experience (B 294 and B 359).

In the third *Critique* Kant says that the understanding (in part) prescribes the laws that reason uses as a basis, *a priori,* to nature. In any event it is the understanding that enables us to *think* the object of sensible intuition (A 51/B 75) by giving unity to the pure synthesis of the imagination according to *a priori* rules. These *a priori* rules are the categories, underlying all of this of course are the *a priori* iterations of space and time which ground (by giving a rule to) all sensible intuitions.

Knowledge or cognition occurs when the manifold of intuition is combined by the imagination under a concept given by the understanding through its unifying pure concepts of synthesis, the categories. But when the cognitive powers are brought into play by the presentation of a beautiful object, no determinate concept restricts them to a particular rule of cognition. The cognitive powers are in a free play (*freirs Spiel*). The under-standing and the imagination are in a free play because there is no determinate concept to restrict them to a particular rule of cognition. This mental state must be a feeling (*Gefühl*), the mind is aware of the free play of the imagination and the understanding although it cannot subsume this awareness under a concept and obtain actual *knowledge* of it. This free play of the cognitive powers must be universally communi-cable, since it is only reference to cognition (in general) that a presentation can be made that holds for everyone. The cognitive powers in their free play harmonize as they refer the given presentation to cognition in general, and cognition in general provides the universal reference point around which we can expect the cognitive powers of any similarly constituted subject whatever to harmonize as well.

I would like to make two comments: 1. The mental state accompanying the presentation of an object which we call beautiful is a *feeling*. We feel the free play of the imagination and the understanding. We feel the mind's *freedom* when we are in the presence of the beautiful, we get a sense of *timelessness* as well. We feel our freedom from the constraints of time, the condition of inner sense. This is not an awareness of a concept, it is a feeling of freedom. For Kant, self-consciousness or apperception too is free from the constraints of space and time. It could be argued that the causal principle of freedom is epistemologically but not ontologically privileged (see Henry E Allison, *Kant's Theory of Freedom*, Cambridge, 1990). 2. It would not be incompatible with the argument if we say that through the aesthetic experience we get a *sense* of timelessness in terms of our intelligible character as moral agents. Feeling is something we experience in the spatio-temporal empirical world, yet we feel things that transcend space and time when in the presence of the beautiful. Compare Louis MacNeice's *Meeting Point*:

> Time was aware and she was here
> And life no longer what it was,
> The bell was silent in the air
> And all the room aglow because
> Time was away and she was here.

Or, Rabindranath's

> Time is endless in thy hands, my lord
> There is none to count thy minutes
> Days and nights pass and ages bloom
> And fade like flowers.
> Thou knowest how to wait.
> Thy centuries follow each other
> Perfecting a small wild flower. (*Gitanjali*, no. LXXXII)

We *experience* the transcendent, noumenal world when we feel the free play of the cognitive powers. It appears that we have access to the super-sensible that does not depend upon the postulates of pure practical reason.

Is Kant's argument persuasive? He should have asked: *is* the free play of the cognitive powers accompanying the presentations of the beautiful a universally communicable mental state that is valid for everyone? Or, is it *necessarily* communicable? Kant's language suggests the latter question.

4

The Phenomenon Called Beauty

THE presentation that occurs in a judgement of taste has subjective universal communicability without presupposing a determinate concept. This is the communication of the mental state that exists or obtains when the imagination and the understanding are in free play, in so far as they harmonize with each other as required for cognition in general. We should note the fact that the imagination and the understanding do not always harmonize. The feeling of the sublime results from a tension between the two cognitive powers. Is the experience of the beautiful an exceptional phenomenon? The subjective relation of harmony between the cognitive powers required for cognition in general must hold for everyone. It must be communicable as any determinate cognition, since the subjective condition of any cognition rests on the relation between the cognitive powers. The determinate cognition arises when the synthesis of intuition of the manifold by the imagination under a concept of understanding occurs. How is a mental state communicable without a concept? Kant appears to get around this problem by referring the mental state to "cognition in general," which he holds is somehow objective in the sense that the minds of more than one subject can refer to it. Kant would also say (and in fact he does) that the *ability* to communicate one's mental state carries with it a pleasure. This can be established empirically and psychologically. But the explanation of the ability itself is yet to be given.

There is of course our natural propensity of sociability. But the pleasure of making a judgement of taste is something more than this pleasure. That pleasure has to necessarily occur when one is in the presence of the object we judge beautiful. It is as if beauty were a characteristic of object, determined according to concepts, even though beauty is no empirical predicate, nothing in itself apart from a reference to the subject's *feeling*. In Hume's celebrated phrase it resides in the eye of the beholder. How is it possible to communicate that which is nothing in itself apart from a feeling in a subject? Kant thinks that such communication is possible. Instead of explaining the "how" of the question, he is more concerned with establishing whether and how aesthetic judgements are possible *a priori*.

In making a judgement of taste we are said to be conscious of a reciprocal subjective harmony of the two cognitive powers. We feel the mental state. Is this consciousness *passive*. The original meaning of *aesthetic* is related to sense perception (from the Greek *aisthesthai*) or *active* (intellectual)? Kant's answer would be that the consciousness of harmony of the cognitive powers is the result of an active mental process, but the feeling of pleasure and displeasure to which a judgement of taste is referred cannot be intellectual. It could have been so if the presentation that prompts the judgement of taste were a concept. It so happens in the case of the objective schematism of judgements in the first *Critique* (A 137/B176). Judgements such as these are not in reference to feelings, and hence not judgements of taste. A judgement of taste determines the object with regard to liking and the predicate of beauty. Hence it is only through *sensation* that the mind can be aware of the unity of the relation in the subject between imagination and understanding. The sensation quickens or animates the two cognitive powers to an indeterminate activity. The activity is in accordance with that required for cognition in general. An objective relation can only be thought, but in so far as it has subjective conditions it can be sensed in the effect it has on the mind. If the relation is not based on a concept, the *only* way we become conscious of it is through a sensation of this relation's effect. What is meant by the relation's effect is the facilitated play of the imagination and the understanding enlivened (*beleben*) by their reciprocal harmony. This harmony is necessary for cognition in general. The presentation of this harmony accords with the conditions of universality. The cognitive powers are brought into the proportioned attune-ment (*proportionale stimmung*) required for all cognition. As human beings we judge by means of understanding combined with the senses. So the attunement is considered valid for all of us. We can therefore expect that any human being in the presence of an object which occasions the mental state to associate with the beautiful will experience the same sensation. The beautiful, then, is liked universally without a concept.

To put the matter in short, beauty is a subjective mental state since it is the result of the free play of the cognitive powers and we may expect the same mental state to occur in any subject endowed with the same powers. Hence, the mental state is communicable by presenting another subject with the object that occasioned the mental state. It is only in this way the experience of beauty is objective. Through the free play of the cognitive powers the mind is aware of its freedom. Through the contemplation of the beautiful, over which we "linger" (*weilen*), the mind experiences a sense of timelessness.

What is it in the object that precipitates the free play of the cognitive powers? It is nothing more than the way the object is presented or what Kant calls the form of purposiveness. The judgement of taste is based on the form of purposiveness of an object.

Purposiveness or *forma finalis* (purposive form) is the causality that a concept has with regard to its object. A purpose

(*Zweck*) is the object of a concept where the concept is regarded as the real basis of the object's possibility. We think of a purpose when we think of the form or existence of the object itself as an effect that is only possible through a concept of that effect. To say, we think of a purpose when we think of the existence or form of a tree is being possible only through some cause having the concept of "tree." An analogous issue obtains in Indian philosophy concerning the debate on the *vyakti, jati* and *akṛti* between Nyāya and Mimāṁsā. Kant's notion of *causality* of a concept parallels fairly to *shakti* residing in a noun like "cow." Thinking "tree" involves thinking what a tree is *for*. The causality that the concept "tree" has with regard to the object that is a tree is purposiveness, i.e., the existence of the tree is thought as being the result of some purpose contained in the concept "tree."

The will, says Kant, is the power of desire which acts in conformity with the presentation of a purpose. However, we call objects, states of mind or acts purposive even if their possibility does not necessarily presuppose the presentation of a purpose. We explain them by assuming that they are based on a causality that operates according to purposes. Hence, there can be purposiveness without a purpose. We do not claim to know the cases of such purposive form in a will, but we cannot grasp the explanation of its possibility unless we have a will. We can observe a purposiveness as to form and take note of this purposive form in objects without basing the purposiveness on a purpose, which would require knowledge of the concept.

To explain this further we may note that a judgement of taste cannot be based on a subjective purpose, that is, purpose regarded as the basis of liking. Such a liking is based on agreeableness, and always involves an interest in the existence of the object of pleasure. Neither can the judgement be determined by a presentation of an objective purpose, that is, a presentation of the object itself as possible in terms of connection to some other purpose. An objective purpose involves a concept of the good. The aesthetic judgement of taste involves only the relation of the presentational powers, Kant seems to use "presentational power" and "cognitive power" interchangeably to refer to imagination and understanding. It is expected of Kant that he should use "understanding" to be a cognitive rather than a presentational power. Intuition and imagination are undoubtedly presentational powers, while "cognitive powers" refer to imagination and understanding. The use of different terms may be taken to indicate a subtlety. Kant does not say explicitly what the presentational powers are, on p. 61 of Pluhar's translation, "imagination and understanding" is inserted after "presentational powers." So the free play of the presentational powers become equivalent to saying the free play of the cognitive powers, i.e., imagination and understanding. The same powers are referred to in both cases, but the different terms refer to their different functions as presentational or cognitive, depending on their employment, to one another as they are determined by a presentation of an object the judgement determines as beautiful. This relation of the presentational powers is connected to the feeling of a pleasure which the judgement of taste declares to be valid for everyone. The universal communicability of the feeling that accompanies the presentation of certain objects is empirical for what is beautiful. This suggests that such a taste stems from a deeply hidden basis common to all human beings that underlines their agreement in judging the forms under which objects are given.

The judgement of taste cannot be based on the agreeableness accompanying the presentations, or a presentation of the object's perfection (which involves the concept of the good). An aesthetic judgement based on charm or the agreeable character of an object is empirical. An aesthetic judgement that asserts an object to be beautiful is pure. Only pure (formal) aesthetic judgements are in fact not the proper judgements of taste, it can only be the "subjective purposiveness" in the presentation of the object without any purpose (subjective or objective) that determines the judgement of taste. The subject is conscious of a purposiveness that does not depend on agreeableness or a concept of the good. The subject is conscious of "purposiveness without a purpose" and so is the *mere form* of purposiveness in the presentation by which the object is given to us.

The feeling of pleasure accompanying the free play of the cognitive powers is a merely contemplative pleasure. It is the consciousness of a merely formal purposiveness in the play accompanying the presentation of an object. This consciousness contains a basis for determining the subject's activity regarding the enlivening of his cognitive powers. The consciousness in an aesthetic judgement, then, provides an inner causality that is purposive with regard to cognition in general, it is not restricted to a determinate cognition. The consciousness contains the mere form of the subjective purposiveness of a presentation. The pleasure is not practical in any way, since there is no input from either a pathological basis (agreeableness) or an intellectual basis (the concept of the good). It has a causality in it, however, it keeps the cognitive powers engaged in their occupation without any further aim beyond the contemplation of the presentation itself. We linger in our contemplation of the beautiful because this contemplation reinforces and reproduces itself. The mind is actively engaged in this contemplative pleasure, enjoying the free play of the cognitive powers.

It would not be inappropriate to say that Kant's position is that the mind is aware of a sense of *timelessness* in this contemplation. It is this awareness, which is not cognitive, that makes the truly beautiful object endlessly fascinating.

Hence the mental state we experience in the presence of an object which we call beautiful is the result of the mind's awareness of its freedom and the possibility of a world that exists beyond the constraints of time. The aesthetic experience Kant describes is a consciousness, a non–cognitive awareness, of the super-sensible.

How can we support this claim?

In his General comment on the First Division of the Analytic (of the Beautiful), Kant defines taste as an ability to judge an object in reference to the "free lawfulness of the imagination." In a judgement of taste the imagination must be considered in its freedom. Its power in this context is productive and spontaneous, as opposed to reproductive. In apprehending a given object of sense the imagination does *not* have free play, since it is tied to the determinate form of the sensed object. But the object may offer the imagination as just the sort of form in the combination of its manifold so that the imagination would design in harmony with the understanding's lawfulness if it were left to itself and free.

Does it makes sense to say that the imagination is free, autonomous and lawful in itself? Only the understanding provides a law. When the imagination must proceed according to a determinate law, i.e., the categories, its product is determined by concepts. If the liking is determined by concepts, it is a liking for the good and not the beautiful. It is only a lawfulness without a law (the form of lawfulness itself) and a subjective harmony of the imagination and the understanding without an objective harmony (which would result in a cognition) that is compatible with the free lawfulness of the understanding (the free lawfulness of the understanding has also been called purposiveness without a purpose. See *Judgement*, section 22, page 78 of the Bernard translation) and the peculiarity of a judgement of taste. Here the form of lawfulness itself is compared to the form of purposiveness itself, the imagination is free and active in the judgement of taste. The mind is conscious of its freedom.

A presentation of freedom is the *sine qua non* of any beautiful object. Our experience of the beautiful, the mental state, is freedom. And that is why we feel inclined to linger on it. Whatever lacks the elements bores us. Anything that shows still regularity runs counter to taste, it does not allow us to enjoy the contemplation of it for any length of time. On the contrary, whatever lends itself to unstudied and purposive play by the imagination is always new to us.

> A thing of beauty is a joy for ever (Keats)
>
> Hold infinity in the palm of one's hand
> And eternity in an hour (Blake)

Kant's example of the song of a bird as offering to our taste than human song hits off the mark. Kant thinks that the song of a bird, since it cannot be brought under a rule of music, seems to contain freedom. There are two instances against Kant's thesis. First is Beethoven, who was much inspired by Kant's third *Critique*, and he considered his own musical creations as assertions of creative freedom. Another is Rabindranath, who in his poem *Balākā* says that birds have been given songs, they go on repeating it. To man was given voice, in singing, he gives out more than what was given to him by Nature.

We never get tired of looking at such object, the merely contemplative pleasure reinforces and reproduces itself without limit. Through this state of mind we relish a sense of timelessness and freedom. We become aware, through a consciousness, and so experience the super-sensible. The aesthetic experience is a doorway to the noumenal.

5

Kant's Concept of Art

FREEDOM is also the *sine qua non* condition of arts. We hardly call anything art except a production through freedom, i.e., a production through a power of choice that bases its acts on reason. Nature then does not produce art. If we posit God we could regard nature as a production of power of choice, *devasya kavyam,* as it were. Art is distinguished from science and craft, art is not something we are able to do as soon as we understand the rules. It is a free spirit, *Geist,* that animates a work of art. Considering art in general, Kant distinguishes mechanical art from aesthetic art. Mechanical art makes a possible object actual adequately to our cognition of the object. We recognize it, but get no pleasure from it. Art that intends to arouse in us a feeling of pleasure is aesthetic art, which comprises agreeable art and fine art. Art is agreeable if its purpose is that the pleasure should accompany presentations that are mere sensations. Art is fine if its purpose is that the pleasure should accompany presentations that are ways of cognizing. Fine art is a way of presenting that is purposive without a purpose and furthers culture of our mental powers to facilitate social communication. The standard of fine art is the reflective power of judgement rather than the power of sensation.

Natural beauty *is* a beautiful thing, artistic beauty is a beautiful *presentation* of a thing, not necessarily a *beautiful* thing. It could well be said that fine art describes beautifully what we find in nature to be disagreeable or ugly. The beautiful presentation of an object is actually only the form of a concept's exhibition by which the concept is universally communicated. Although we are conscious that fine art is art and not a product of nature, the purposiveness in its form must seem *free* from all constraints of chosen rules just *as if* it were a product of nature (compare the first formulation of the categorical imperative. "Act *as if* the maxim of your action were to become through your will a universal law of nature.") This is necessary if the presentation is to evoke the feeling of freedom in the play of our cognitive powers that results from the mental state and we call art beautiful. Although the purposiveness in a product of fine art is intentional, it must not *seem* intentional. Fine art must look like nature even though we know it is art. This is because it is nature that presents us with purposiveness without a purpose. Nature appears to be purposiveness but we cannot know if in fact it is purposive, much less what the purpose *is*. Purposiveness without a purpose (lawfulness without a law) presents the ***form*** of purposiveness that enlivens the cognitive powers in their free play and produces the feeling of pleasure we experience when in the presence of the beautiful. Genius is the talent that can give a rule that looks like freedom to fine art. In the context of Kant's aesthetics, spirit or *Geist* is the ability to exhibit aesthetic ideas. Aesthetic ideas may be called unexpoundable presentations (*inexponible Vorstellung*) of the imagination in its free play. And in this way they are like ideas of reason.

Spirit or *Geist* is the ability that genius has in order to express aesthetic ideas in such a way that they may communicate the mental attainment the ideas produce. An aesthetic idea is a presentation of the imagination that prompts much thought, but to which no determinate thought or concept whatsoever can be adequate. As aesthetic idea strives towards something that lies beyond the bounds of experience. They are inner intuitions to which no concept can be completely adequate. In the process of creating aesthetic ideas we feel freedom from the law of association under which the imagination operates in its empirical use. An aesthetic idea is a presentation that makes us add to a concept the thoughts of much that is ineffable, but the feeling which quickens (*beleben*) our cognitive powers, connecting language with spirit. Fine art exhibits aesthetic ideas, when it does so successfully, we say it is beautiful. We never get tired of contemplating it, it gives us a sense of the free and timeless aspects of our nature.

6

The Beautiful and the Moral

KANT connects the beautiful to the super-sensible through the moral. In section 59 of the *Critique of Judgement* he takes up explicitly the topic of the relationship between aesthetics and morality and makes the beautiful the symbol of morality.

The judgement of taste is disinterested. In saying that something is beautiful we do not, rather must not, have any interest in determining its basis. Yet, *after* the judgement been made on purely aesthetic grounds an interest can be connected with it, of course indirectly. This interest can be empirical or intellectual. By *empirical* interest Kant meant that the interest is based on some inherent inclination of human nature. By "intellectual" he meant that the interest is based on the will's property of being determinable *a priori* by reason, or the will's moral property. The point is that once the judgement of taste is made on the basis of the form of purposiveness without a purpose, the liking can then be connected to a pleasure in the existence of the object. It is worth recalling that for Kant interest consists in pleasure or satisfaction in the existence of an object. The argument that the aesthetic judgement is related to our moral interest is then supportable.

The beautiful can only be of empirical interest in society. On our part there is the inherent inclination to society, which is furthered by sociability, which in turn is enhanced by taste. Taste is an ability to judge whatever allows us to communicate our feeling to everyone else, and this ability enhances our fitness and propensity for society. That something is beautiful is no private judgement like "This is beautiful to me." Our refinement consists in having the inclination and the skill to communicate our pleasure to others. We expect a concern for universal communication of pleasure on the basis of our very humanity. Taste is a kind of common sense (*sensus communis*) which is accomplished by putting ourselves in the position of everyone else and comparing our judgements to the merely possible judgements of others. This can be done by leaving out as much as possible of the material or sensation from the presentational state which precipitates our judgement and paying attention only to its formal features. When we do this we expect agreement from everyone, i.e., any being possessing similar mental faculties (Bhavabhuti hoped for finding a *samāna dharma* in the immensity of time and space). As civilization evolves, in place of charms, beautiful forms overtake in importance, and refined taste is marked by the principle of universal communicability in fine art. Charms or sensations are valued in art only to the extent they are universally communicable. The point however is that through our natural inclination to society an indirect empirical interest in the beautiful is possible. In his *Lectures on Metaphysics*, Kant had remarked that taste is the faculty of judging through satisfaction or dissatisfaction, according to communal and universally valid sense.

We may now state what could be said to be *the problem of the third Critique* and what lies in his seeking a transition from the sensible to the super-sensible. The attachment of the beautiful to our inclination to society is empirical, hence our interest in the beautiful based on this inclination can provide only an ambiguous transition from the agreeable to the good. If we consider a judgement of taste in its pure form, we may discover something that has reference to it *a priori*, if only indirectly. That is, we may discover an intellectual interest in the beautiful. If such an interest were to reveal itself, taste would reveal how our ability to make judgements of taste provide a transition from sense enjoyment to moral feeling. Does Kant equate the good with the super-sensible? Kant defines the good in the third *Critique* as presupposing objective purposiveness which requires the concept of a purpose, either in terms of what the thing is meant to be, or the completeness any thing may have as a thing of its kind. Neither "purpose" in this sense, nor "perfection" are objects of any possible experience. They are ideas of reason, which always concern the super-sensible. A rational idea can never become cognition because it contains a concept of the super-sensible to which no adequate intuition can ever be given.

Kant's manner of argument suggests that it is possible to use taste purposively to promote moral feeling and to show that judgement is a mediating unit in the chain of our *a priori* powers upon which all legislation depend. By demonstrating an intellectual, i.e., *a priori* interest in the beautiful, Kant finds a link between the agreeable and the good, or the sensible and the super-sensible. The intellectual interest is *a priori* in the sense that the interest is free from all inclinations or empirical elements. Not, of course, in the sense of *a priori* coming *before* the judgement of taste, which remains disinterested. To say this is to suggest that judgement is the mediating link between the understanding (the proper application of which is the giving of rules to our experience of nature, i.e., the sensible), and reason (the application of which is to provide principles for the use of our freedom, i.e., the super-sensible). In the judgement of taste we *experience* this link to the super-sensible through feeling, rather than merely postulating the super-sensible as a necessary consequence of pure practical reason. The value and importance of feeling finds an eloquent expression in Goethe's *Faust*:

Give it what name you will.
Your joy, love, heart, your God
For me, I have no name
To give it, feeling's surely all
Names are but noise and smoke,
Obscuring heavenly light

—*Faust*, Part I Martha's Garden,
tr. Phillip Wayne, Penguin, 1963

The connection of the beautiful to the moral is not new to Kant. It was there with Plato, Shaftesbury, Wolff, Baumgarten and Meir (for the Greeks the word *kalon* meant both *beautiful* and *good*. Compare the Sanskrit *kalyāna* as a cognate of *kalon,* which Aristotle uses along with *agathos.* The Sanskrit *kalyānī* implies both virtuous and charming. Shiva in the south Indian parlance is *kalyanasundara.* A hermeneutics of Rabindranath's poem *Tapobhanga* is possible along this line of thought. The Sanskrit word *śubham,* meaning the auspicious, has an affinity with the word *śobhana,* meaning *becoming,* while its feminine, *śobhana* meaning comedy or charming) who have conceived interest in the beautiful as a sign of good moral character. Others have of course pointed out that persons with taste are found to be vain, obstinate, given to ruinous passions and so feelings can hardly be associated with good moral characters. Whatever this counter example may indicate, the fact that stands out is that the beautiful is distinct in kind from moral feeling, and it may prove impossible to reconcile the beautiful with moral interest by an allied intrinsic affinity between the two. Nevertheless the feeling of the beautiful is connected to moral feeling. To take a direct interest in the beautiful forms of nature (not nature's charms, which are empirical) is a mark of a good soul. If this interest is associated with the contemplation of nature, then at least a mental attunement favourable to moral feeling will be indicated. By *direct interest* Kant meant a liking for nature's product for its form and its existence even though no charm of sense is involved. (The liking for nature's products for its form and existence might serve the purposes of ecology.) The interest is direct but remains intellectual.

We have in the aesthetic power of judgement an ability to judge forms without using concepts, in which we feel a liking that we also make a rule for everyone, even though the judgement is not based on an interest and does not in itself give rise to one. We also have an intellectual power of judgement, which is an ability of determining *a priori* the mere forms of practical maxims of the liking of which we make a law for everyone.

The pleasure or displeasure in the first judgement is that of taste, of the second judgement it is that of moral feeling. Moral feeling causes reason to have a direct interest in the objective reality of its ideas. The mind cannot contemplate the beauty of nature without having its interest aroused. This interest in the beauty of nature shares a kinship with the moral. Actually, Kant endeavours to show, there is no conflict between moral interest and a disinterested liking for the beautiful. The beautiful and the moral are connected through the interest in the reality of its ideas. While the empirical interest in the beautiful is indirect, the intellectual interest is direct. Both interests are only *indirectly* connected to the judgement of taste. Nature displays itself as art, i.e., nature seems to us to display itself in terms of a lawful arrangement and not merely as the result of chance. Nature displays itself as purposiveness without a purpose, which is the form of the beautiful. Since we do not find this purpose anywhere outside us, we look for it in ourselves. We look for it in that which constitutes the ultimate purpose of our existence.

7

Beauty as a Symbol of Morality

KANT makes a more explicit connection between the moral and the beautiful in Section 59 of the third *Critique*. Let us ask, what does Kant mean by "Symbol"? A symbol is analogous to what he called a "schema" in the first *Critique*. Intuitions are required to establish that our concepts have reality. If the concepts are empirical, the intuitions are called "examples." If the concepts are pure concepts of the understanding, the intuitions conveyed by means of the imagination and which are therefore abstract are called "schemata." A schema is what mediates and so makes possible the subsumption of intuitions under concepts of the understanding or a schema is what makes possible the application of concepts of the understanding to intuitions. It does so by sharing features of both a concept and an intuition (A137-47/B176-87). But no intuition can be adequate to a rational concept (an idea of reason), and so we cannot establish their objective reality for the sake of theoretical cognition. All "hypotyposis" or exhibition consists in making a concept sensible and it is either "schematic" or "symbolic." It could be said that for Kant schema and symbol are interpretative devices derived from imagination, and without which no cognition in general would be possible at all. In schematic hypotyposis a concept of the understanding is formed and the intuition corresponding to it is given *a priori*. In symbolic hypotyposis there is a concept which only reason can think to which no *sensible* intuition can be adequate. This concept is supplied with an intuition that judgement treats in a way that is only analogous to the procedure it follows in schematizing. The treatment of this intuition agrees with the procedure of uniting a concept of the understanding with a sensible intuition merely in the rule followed rather than in terms of the intuition itself. Kant's question is how to provide objective reality for pure concepts of Understanding and Reason? And he says that when the concept cannot be represented immediately (as is the case with a rational concept), but only indirectly or mediately through its implications or consequences the act of exhibition may be called the symbolization of the concept. In fact, concepts of the sensible are schematized, and the concepts of the super-sensible are symbolized. The latter is an aid or expedient we use for concepts of the super-sensible (ideas of reason) which as such cannot be exhibited and given in every possible experience, but which necessarily belong to knowledge, even if only possible in practical knowledge. The symbol of an idea (or concept of reason) is a presentation of the object by analogy. We present the object of the idea (e.g., God) in terms of the relation which some other object (e.g., human being) has to its effects or consequences and which is the same relation that we consider the object itself as having to its consequences, even though the objects themselves are of wholly different order. (Rudolf Otto has wonderfully worked out the Kantian motion of schema in his *The Idea of the Holy,* the *tremendum* is schematized "justice," the *fascinans* by "goodness" or "love," and the *mysterium* by "absoluteness." See the chapter "The Holy as an A Priori Category," *The Idea of the Holy,* tr. John W. Harver, Penguin Books, 1959. On this issue Rudolf Makkreel's *Imagination and Interpretation in Kant: The Hermeneutical Import of the Critique of Judgement,* Chicago University Press, 1990 is worth pursuing.) For example, we may present organized things in nature to their cause as we present a clock in relation to its human maker. The relation of each to causality in general as a category is the same in both cases. The intrinsic character of the subject that has this relation and these effects remains unknown, we cannot exhibit it, we can only exhibit the relation.

Symbolic presentation is a *kind* of intuitive presentation. It is not to be *contrasted* to intuitive presentation. Intuitive presentation are either schematic or symbolic. Both are exhibitions or hypotyposes and not mere characterizations or designations of concepts by sensible signs. Hence, all intuitions supplied for *a priori* concepts are either schemata or symbols. Schemata contain direct exhibitions of the object, symbols contain indirect exhibitions of the object. Schematic exhibition is demonstrative, symbolic exhibition uses an analogy (for which we use empirical intuitions as well). Judgement performs a double function in symbolic exhibition: it applies the concept to the object of a sensible intuition, and then it applies the rule by which it reflects on that intuition to an entirely different object, of which the former object is only the symbol. The symbolic exhibition (hypotyposis) expresses concepts not by means of a direct intuition but only according to an analogy with one. The symbolic exhibition is a transfer of our reflection on an object of intuition to an entirely different concept to which perhaps no intuition can ever directly correspond. If we may call a mere way of presenting a cognition, which is permissible for determining an object *practically,* then all our cognition of God is symbolic, i.e., cognition by analogy (Paul Tillich's thesis that religious language is symbolic may have had its source in Kant. Kant also says that whoever omits everything intuitive falls into deism which allows us to cognize nothing whatsoever, not even from a practical point of view. And whoever regards or cognition of God as schematic falls into anthropomorphism. And it was against the deists' pretensions that Kant directed his critiques of the theistic proofs. We may also add, whoever regards cognition of God as schematic is on the way to fundementalism.)

With this understanding of "symbol" in place, Kant asserts that the beautiful is the symbol of the morally good, and hence we refer the beautiful to the morally good. This is what we all do naturally, and require others to do as duty. Our liking includes a claim to everyone else's assent. The mind is conscious of being enabled by this reference to rise above a mere receptivity of pleasure derived from sense impressions. The morally good is the *intelligible* that is in view. In Section 57 Kant explains that pure reason falls into three kinds of antinomy corresponding to the three mental powers of cognition, the feeling of pleasure and displeasure and the power of desire. Each of the three cognitive powers (understanding, judgement and reason) have its *a priori* principles (lawfulness, purposiveness and final purpose, respectively). When reason passes judgement on these *a priori* principles and their use, it demands the unconditioned for every given conditioned, which we can never find if we regard the sensible as representing things in themselves. Three antinomies arise: for the cognitive power, an antinomy of reason concerning the theoretical use of the understanding when this use is extended up to the unconditioned; antinomy of reason for the feeling of pleasure and displeasure concerning the aesthetic use of judgement; and for the power of desire, an antinomy of reason concerning the practical use of our intrinsically legislative reason. All of these antinomies are alike in a sense that they force reason to abandon the otherwise very natural presupposition that objects of sense are things in themselves. Reason is forced to regard objects of sense as mere appearances that are based on a supersensible substrate, the concept of which is only an idea and precludes cognition proper. Interestingly, Kant remarks that if there were no such antinomy, reason could never bring itself to accept such a principle that so greatly narrows the area in which it can speculate.

The solution to all three antinomies is to rely on the assumption of a supersensible substrate for the given objects, taking the latter as appearances only. The sensible must be regarded as only the mere appearance of things based on an intelligible substrate of nature outside and within us. This intelligible (but not sensible) substrate should be taken as the thing itself. When we do this we are led to three ideas, the idea of the supersensible in general as the substrate of nature, second, the idea of the same supersensible considered as the principle of nature's subjective purposiveness for our cognitive power, and third, the idea of the same supersensible regarded as the principle of the purposes of freedom and of the harmony of these purposes in the moral sphere. It should be noticed that Kant does at times come close to sounding like a Hegelian idealist. Patrick Riley (as Zammito adduces in his *the Genesis of Kant's Critique of Judgement,* the University of Chicago Press, 1992) has argued the view in Section 57 and comments that Kant is approaching Hegel in recognizing the reality of reason.

The principle of nature's subjective purposiveness for our cognitive power is what Kant has in mind when he says that the morally good is the intelligible that taste has in view. It is with this intelligible, the morally good, that our higher cognitive powers harmonize, and without it contradictions would continually arise from the contrast between the nature of these powers and the claims that taste makes. In other words, the antinomy of taste will arise.

Kant offers four points of the analogy between the beautiful and the morally good, First, we like the beautiful directly but not in its concept, rather we like the beautiful directly upon reflecting on the intuition. We like the morally good directly in its concept. Secondly, we like the beautiful without any interest, and while our liking for the morally good is necessarily connected with an interest, the interest does *not precede* our judgement about the liking, it is produced *by* the liking.

Thirdly, in judging the beautiful we present the freedom of the imagination and hence the freedom of our power of sensibility as harmonizing with the lawfulness of the understanding. In a moral judgement we think of the freedom of the will as the will's harmony with itself according to universal laws of reason. Finally, we present the subjective principle for judging the beautiful as universal, i.e., vaild for everyone, but as unknowable through any universal concept. The morally good we also declare to be universally valid for all subjects through its objective principle, which we also declare to be knowable through a universal concept (the form of law as such). Moral judgements are capable of having determinate constitutive principles, and the possibility of a moral judgement depends on our basing moral maxims on those principles and their universality. The beautiful object become an indirect, that is, analogous, presentation of a good will. Through this analogous presentation of the concept of a good will, the pleasure we experience in the presence of the beautiful becomes an experience of the intelligible moral world, a world which practical reason can only postulate. The aesthetic experience of the beautiful has metaphysical significance for Kant.

The beautiful, then, is analogous to the morally good. Kant is not saying that the beautiful *is* morally good, only that the beautiful is *like* the morally good. It symbolizes the morally good, the experience of the beautiful is like the moral experience. Additional evidence of this is that the names that we use to describe beautiful objects seem to presuppose that we judge the objects morally. Beautiful objects arouse sensations in us that are somehow analogous to the consciousness we have in a mental state produced by moral judgements. The judgement of taste, in reference to the beautiful, is significant to Kant's moral metaphysics in the sense that it provides us with a transition from the sensible to the supersensible realm of the morally good. It is not for nothing that the logical form of Kant's account of the beautiful and a good will paralleled each other (see Ted Cohen's essay "Why Beauty is a Symbol of Morality" in *Essays in Kant's Aesthetics,* ed. Ted Cohen and Paul Guyer, Chicago University Press, 1982).

8

The Sublime
How the Sublime Differs from the Beautiful?

THE aesthetic judgement described under the Analytic of the Beautiful is relevant to Kant's moral metaphysics, but indirectly. The relations between the mental state that we experience in the presence of the beautiful is only analogously like the morally good, beauty is a symbol of morality. We get a sense of timelessness and of our freedom when we experience through a mental state the free play of the cognitive powers and the contemplative pleasure that reinforces and reproduces itself without limit when we are presented with an object which we call beautiful. While the experiences are real, they provide only an indirect pathway to the noumenal. In the Analytic of the Sublime, the connection between the sensible and the super-sensible is direct. The sublime (*das Erhabene*) is "what even the ability to *think* proves that the mind has a power surpassing any standard of sense."

The Analytic of the Sublime in the third *Critique* not only completes the architectonic articulation of aesthetic judgements, but also demonstrates a connection between the aesthetic experience in general and the ultimate nature of the self. Kant himself called this part a critique of spiritual feeling.

We may first note the similarities between the beautiful and the sublime. We like them both for their own sake, and they both presuppose that we make a judgement of reflection rather than a judgement of sense or a logically determinative one. Our liking for the sublime, as in the case of the beautiful, does not depend on a sensation such as that of the agreeable, nor does it depend on a determinate concept as does our liking for the good. We do refer the liking to concepts, although it is indeterminate which concepts they are. The liking in both the beautiful and the sublime is connected with the mere exhibition or power of exhibition, namely the imagination, understanding and reason that comprise the power of concepts, and the harmony of these faculties and the imagination (understanding in reference to the beautiful and reason in reference to the sublime) furthers their aims. This harmony is also the basis for the universal validity of the singular (subjective) judgements we make regarding the beautiful and the sublime.

Now we note the differences: The beautiful concerns the form of the object. The beautiful object presents the form of purposiveness, without presenting a purpose. The form of the object we judge beautiful must be bounded in some way. If it were *boundless* there would be no form, and hence no apparent purposiveness. The sublime, on the other hand, must be found in a formless object. The sublime is a presentation of unboundedness, either as in the object or because the object prompts us to present unboundedness as we add to this unboundedness the *thought* of its totality. The beautiful is an exhibition of an indeterminate concept of the understanding. The sublime is an exhibition of an indeterminate concept of *reason*. Our liking for the beautiful is connected to a presentation of *quality*, our liking for the sublime is connected to a presentation of *quantity*. Kant's analytics of the beautiful and the sublime follow the table of categories presented in the first *Critique*, the four main divisions of which are quality, quantity, relation and modality (See Paul Guyer, "Kant's Distinction between the Beautiful and the Sublime," *Review of*

Metaphysics, 35.4 June, 1982). The liking for the beautiful carries with it a direct feeling of life's being furthered, and so it is compatible with charms and with an imagination at play. The liking for the sublime, on the other hand, is a pleasure that arises only indirectly, it is produced by the feeling of a momentary inhibition of the vital forces followed immediately by an outpouring of them that is all the more stronger. The liking for the sublime is an emotion (*Ruhrung*) which seems to be seriousness rather than play in the activity of the imagination. In liking the sublime, the mind is always alternately attracted and repelled by the object at the same time. There is a tension between harmony and violence (Cf. Rudolf Otto's description of The Holy as *tremendum* as well as *fascinans*). It is not so much a positive pleasure as it is a feeling of admiration and respect. It could be called a negative pleasure. In these ways the sublime departs from the beautiful. The contrast between the two finds an expression in Rabindranath's song:

> Beautiful is thy wristlet, decked with stars and cunningly wrought in myriad-coloured jewels. But more beautiful to me is thy sword formed with its curve of lightening like the outspread wings of the divine bird of Vishnu, prefectly poised in the angry red light of the sunset.
>
> It quivers like the one last response of life in ecstacy of pain at final stroke of death, it shines like the pure flame of being burning up earthly sense with one fierce flash.
>
> Beautiful is thy wristlet, decked with starry gems, but thy sword, O lord of thunder, is wrought with uttermost beauty, terrible to behold or to think of.

(*Gitanjali,* LIII), Yeats' phrase "terrible beauty" may be taken to answer to description of the sublime.

The most important distinction between the beautiful and the sublime concerns the form of the object. Ordinarily beauty carries with it a purposiveness in its form by which the object seems predetermined for our power of judgement. This beauty constitutes in itself an object of our liking. But that which arouses in us a feeling of the sublime may appear in its form *counter-purposive* for our power of judgement, incommensurate with our power of exhibition and violent to our imagination. We cannot perhaps call an object of nature sublime, since "sublime" is a term of approval, and such terms are not properly applied to objects we apprehend as in themselves counterpurposive. All we are entitled to say is that the object is suitable for exhibiting a sublimity that can be *found in the mind;* what is sublime, properly speaking, is not contained in any sensible form but only concerns ideas of reason. The ideas of reason cannot be exhibited adequately, and it is this very inadequacy of the mind to this task that constitutes the feeling of the sublime. The mind's inadequacy to its task can be exhibited in sensibility, i.e., sensible objects can cause the mind to confront this inadequacy through their force or magnitude. The raging ocean is not properly called sublime, but the sight of it attunes the mind to a *feeling* that is sublime. The sublime, then, like the beautiful, is a state of mind. The mind is induced to abandon sensibility and occupy itself with ideas containing a higher purposiveness.

The concept of the sublime in nature indicates nothing purposive in nature itself. The concept of the beautiful, on the contrary, indicates purposiveness involving the very *form* of purposiveness. The concept of sublime indicates to us that there is a purposive *use* to which we can put our intuitions of nature. We *feel* a purposiveness within ourselves entirely independent of nature. We seek a basis outside ourselves for the beautiful in nature, but for the sublime the basis is within ourselves.

9

The Nature of the Sublime

THE state of mind in which we experience the beautiful is one of restful contemplation. The feeling of the sublime is one of mental agitation. We like this mental agitation, and hence, it is judged to be subjectively purposive. The mental state is subjectively purposive because it is only with regard to our mental powers that the given presentation is judged to be purposive (without any purpose or interest). There are two kinds of mental agitation and the imagination refers it to either the cognitive power or the power of desire, depending upon whether the agitation is a "mathematical" or "dynamical" attunement of the mind. And as we attribute the mental state we call the beautiful to the object that occasions it, so we attribute both kinds of mental agitation to the object, presenting it as either mathematically or dynamically sublime.

What we call sublime is absolutely large. To say that something is absolutely large is to say that it is large beyond all comparison. But terms such as large and small are not pure concepts of the understanding, or intuition of sense, or even rational concepts. They must either stand for a concept that belongs to the power of judgement or be derived from such a concept. We need a measure. A magnitude (we can recognize that a thing is a magnitude without any comparison) must be compared to another magnitude if we are to use terms such as large and small. Hence, any determination of the magnitude of appearances can only yield a comparative concept of large or small and not an absolute one.

If we describe something as absolutely large, we imply that the magnitude of the object is superior to that of many other objects of the same kind, but without measuring this superiority determinately. We base our judgement on a standard we assume is the same for everyone, but it is one that serves only for an aesthetic (mere intuition, by the eye) and not a logical (mathematically determinate) judgement of magnitude. Kant argues that all estimation of the magnitude of objects in nature is aesthetic. The magnitude of the basic unit of measurement must be assumed to be known by intuition. It is a subjective standard underlying our reflective judgement about magnitude, which may be empirical or *a priori* (e.g., the magnitude or degree of a certain virtue). We assume this subjective standard to be the same for everyone because the mere magnitude of the object, even if it is considered formless, can carry with it a liking that is universally communicable. This liking involves consciousness of a subjective purposiveness in the use of our cognitive powers. Our liking for the beautiful, expressed in terms of reflective judgement is occasioned by the form of an object, and the liking is purposively attuned in relation to cognition in general. The liking associated with the feeling of the sublime is *not a liking* for the object (which may be formless), it is a liking for the *expansion of the imagination itself.*

When we call something large, absolutely no standard adequate to it can be found outside of it. Such a standard can only be found within it. It is a magnitude equal only to itself. Only an aesthetic estimation can exhibit absolute magnitude, to the extent that the mind can take it in one intuition. From this it follows that the sublime must not be sought in things of nature. The sublime, compared to the rich stimulation that the experience of beauty provides for our study and grasp of nature, is generally fruitless for our understanding of nature. What the sublime illuminates is metaphysics. The sublime is to be found only in our ideas. The sublime is that in comparison to which everything is small and nothing in nature can be such that could not be considered in a different relation as infinitely small. Whatever is given in nature is judged large or small in *comparison* to some measure, and if the measure is changed the judgement of the magnitude changes with it. For example, the immense mountain shrinks into insignificance when compared to the magnitude of the universe revealed through the telescope, and a drop of water is revealed to be a universe through the microscope. Hence no object of the senses is to be called sublime. The sublime is a mental state that occurs when reason sets a task for the imagination that it cannot meet. Reason demands absolute totality as a real idea while the imagination, which is the power of estimating the magnitude of things in the world of sense, can only strive to progress towards infinity. The imagination is inadequate to reasonˆs ideas, and the mind is agitated as a result. The ideas of reason are always either too large or too small for any concept of the understanding. But this inadequacy gives rise in us a feeling that *we have within us a super-sensible power.* What is absolutely large is the use that judgement naturally makes of certain objects so as to arouse in us this feeling that we have super-sensible power, in contrast to this any other use is small. It is not the object that is sublime, then, but the attunement of the mind through a certain presentation that occupies reflective judgement.

The aesthetic judgement of the sublime must be pure, i.e., free of any teleological and hence rational judgement. We must not look for the sublime in products of art such as buildings or monuments, since both the form and maguitude of these are determined by a human purpose. Similarly we must not look for the sublime in natural things, whose very concept carries with it a purpose (which we may not know— purposiveness without a purpose).

Kant understands the sublime as an experience of the noumenal. This is a feeling accompanying a universally communicable mental state. How is this feeling explained? The sublime is based on the expansion of the imagination itself and *not* on the form of the object, as it happens to be the case with the beautiful.

Let us take the case of infinity. The imagination encounters no obstactles when it performs the combination required to present a magnitude. It can progress on its own to infinity guided by numerical concepts provided by the understanding. The imagination provides the schema which mediates and so makes possible the subsumption of the intuitions of the unit of measure under these numerical concepts (for Kant's explanation of schema see the first *Critique,* A 137-47/B176-87). This procedure constitutes the logical estimation of magnitude. Any measuring has a puspose. There is nothing in this measuring that is purposive for or liked by the aesthetic power of judging, or that requires us to comprehend the many successive elements involved in *one* intuition. The imagination is not pushed to its limits. The combination of each quantum is done progressively rather than comprehensively.

On the other hand, reason demands totality for all given magnitudes, comprehension in *one* intuition of all magnitudes, the exhibition of *all* of the members of the progressively increasing numerical series. Not even the infinite escapes this demand of reason. Reason makes us try to think of the infinite as given in its entirety. An infinite given in its entirity can only be an idea of reason. It is this demand of reason that results in the Antinomies, and it is beacuse we try to think of the infinite, either in space or time, or the unconditioned as given in its totality that we ask what is on the other side of it. And here Kant emphasizes the point by stating explicitly that the ability to even *think* the infinite as a whole indicates a mental power that surpasses any standard of sense. To think the infinite as a whole *using* a standard of sense would mean comprehending a unity of some numerical standard to which the infinite could be compared, which is impossible. Thus the fact that the human mind is even able to *think* of a given infinite without contradiction means that it must have within itself a power that is supersensible. This supersensible power yields an idea of a noumena which cannot be intuited but which is regarded as the substrate underlying our intuitions of the world, which are only appearances. With this supersensible power we think of magnitude in terms of a "pure intellectual estimation," which enables us to comprehend the infinite in the world of sense entirely under a concept in spite of the fact that we could never think an infinity in its entirety by means of numerical concepts. Kant speaks here of " supersensible intuition," a power that enables us to think "the infinite of supersensible intuition" as given in our intelligible substrate surpasses any standard of sensibility. This thinking of the infinite of supersensible intuition is not for the sake of some theoretical aim on behalf of our cognitive power, rather, it is an expansion of the mind. Sri Aurobindo speaks of *chitta vistāra.* The Mahayana ethics, and earlier Pali Buddhism had spoken of *brahmavihāra* with allied and somewhat similar intention, through which we *feel* able to cross the barriers of sensibility with a different aim. The different aim that Kant has in mind is the moral. For Kant in the third *Critique* the foremost aspect of our experience of the sublime is that even the very fact that we *have* such an experience that *proves* (*beweist*) there is in us something supersensible. That is to say, the experience of the feeling of the sublime provides tangible evidence that we exist both as sensible and supersensible beings. Such a conclusion is tremendously important for Kant, because this supersensible power of ours is what makes morality possible. If we have no power to transcend the causally determined sensible world, our moral vocation is a no more than a chimera. By pointing to an *experience* that allows us to *feel* our supersensible power, Kant adds another dimension to that connection to the supersensible provided by our awareness of the reality of the moral law. Our awareness of the reality of the moral law is constituted through *feeling,* and this fact itself is important in respect of motivation. My thesis is that the problem of moral motivation in Kant is one of an objectively conceived principle subjectively motivating individual persons.

When the intuition of an appearance in nature carries with it the idea of infinity, we say that nature is sublime. The only way this can occur is when the imagination is unable to take in an object's magnitude. It is only in the aesthetic estimation of magnitude that we feel the strain of the imagination's effort to perform a comprehension that surpasses its ability to encompass the progressive apprehension that a mathematical estimation of magnitude accomplishes easily in a single intuition. The whole of nature includes the possibility of a progression extending to infinity (in space and time), and so the absolute whole of nature as appearance is infinity comprehended. This is contradictory, because an absolute totality of an endless progression is impossible. When the magnitude of a natural object is such that the imagination cannot comprehend it in a single intuition, we are led to the concept of a supersensible substrate. This supersensible substrate is large beyond any standard of sense and makes us judge as sublime not so much the object as the mental attunement in which we find ourselves when we estimate the object. In other words, it is the supersensible substrate (*noumenon*) that is absolutely large and not merely large by comparison, as anything that can be compared to some standard of sense. The object in nature that exceeds the imagination's ability to comprehend it in a single intuition (as opposed to a progressive) occasions in us the feeling of the sublime, which is a mental state of agitation resulting from the imagination's inadequacy to its task. But no object in nature can be truly sublime because if we change our perspective we *can* intuit any object in nature (as appearance) in a single intuition. The only thing that can be absolutely large is the *whole* of nature, which of course involves a contradiction *unless* we think of a supersensible substrate underlying nature as appearance. But only that which is absolutely large is properly called sublime, and so our experience of the feeling of the sublime must ultimately depend on the existence of the supersensible, although the mental state that *is* the sublime, properly speaking, is occasioned by nature as appearance.

10

The Sublime and the Moral

IN JUDGING the beautiful the aesthetic power of judgement refers the imagination in its free play to the understanding. In judging a thing sublime, the aesthetic power of judgement refers the imagination to *reason.* While judging the beautiful, imagination harmonizes with the concepts of the understanding. Though such concepts is left indeterminate when judging the sublime, imagination harmonizes subjectively with the ideas of reason, and such ideas are again left indeterminate.

This harmony of the imagination with reason's ideas produces a mental attunement that conforms to and is compatible with the mental attunement that an influence by determinate practical ideas would produce on feeling. In saying this Kant has in mind the influence of moral ideas or moral feeling. The sense of awe that we experience in the presence of the sublime is very much akin to the sense of awe we experience when we realize that we have a moral vocation.

True sublimity then must be sought only in the mind of the judging person not in the natural object which prompts this mental attunemnt. The mind feels elevated in its own judgement of itself when it contemplates such an object. The mind abandons itself to the imagination and to reason, which has become connected to the imagination without a determinate purpose. This connection expands the mind as it discovers that all the power of the imagination remains inadequate to reason's ideas. We expect universal agreement in our judgement of the sublime, then, on the same basis as that of the beautiful. Since the sublime is a mental state, we expect that any other similarly constituted mind will experience a similar mental state when in the presence of the given object.

The sense of awe that accompanies the feeling of the sublime is akin to the sense of awe that accompanies our realization that we have a moral vocation. Kant bases the liking we feel in judging the sublime on this awe which is based on respect. He defines *respect* in the third *Critique* as the *feeling* that it is beyond our ability to attain an idea that is a law for us. This is his familiar formulation of respect for the *moral* law. But something quite similar takes place when we judge the sublime, as the thought of comprehending in a single intuition the *whole* of nature as appearance. The *whole* of nature as appearance is an idea of reason, which demands the absolute whole. This demand is one that the imagination cannot meet. The imagination's inability to exhibit the idea of reason (in a determinate concept) proves its own limits and inadequacy. Yet the fact that the imagination *tries* to obey the command of reason and make itself adequate to reason's idea *proves* its vocation to obey reason's law (that imagination, our greatest power of sensibility, should strive towards harmony with rational ideas). The feeling of the sublime in nature, then is *respect (Achtung)* for our own vocation. These ideas in the third *Critique* show a striking similarity to the role that awareness of the moral law plays in the second *Critique*. Through this feeling of respect, which is sensible, the superiority of the rational vocation (*Vernuftbestimmung*) of our cognitive powers over the greatest power of sensibility (the imagination), which is intelligible, is made intuitable for us. In his Inaugural Dissertation Kant describes "subreption" as the intellect's trick of slipping in a concept of sense as if it were the concept of an intellectual characteristic. Here respect for the object judged sublime (the concept of sense) is substituted for respect for the ideas of humanity within ourselves (the intellectual concept). The "idea of humanity within ourselves" and the "rational vocation of our cognitive powers" are essentially equivalent formulations for Kant. This "rational vocation" is of course our supersensible *moral* vocation, and we see that in the third *Critique* the feeling of the sublime provides a doorway to the supersensible from the sensible.

The feeling of the sublime is a feeling of displeasure that arises from the imagination's inadequacy, but it is at the same time a pleasure aroused by the fact that the *judgement* that this greatest power of sensibility is inadequate is *itself* in harmony with rational ideas. The judgement is in harmony with the law of reason that requires the imagination to strive to attain an intuition adequate to the idea of reason. The displeasure resulting from the imagination's inadequacy arouses in us the feeling of our supersensible vocation, realizing that every standard of sensibility is inadequate to the ideas of reason is purposive and hence pleasurable. This explains the *agitation* the mind feels when presenting the sublime in nature. The mind feels alternately a repulsion and an attraction to the same object. The judgement itself always remains aesthetic. It is not based on a determinate concept of the object. The judgement presents the subjective play of the mental powers themselves as harmonious by virtue of their contrast. Just as the imagination and the understanding give rise to a subjective purposiveness of the mental powers by accordance when we judge the beautiful, in the same way the conflict or tension between imagination and reason gives rise to a subjective purposiveness when we judge the sublime in that this conflict originates a feeling that we have a power for estimating magnitude (reason) whose superiority cannot be made intuitable by anything other than that power (imagination) which is itself unbounded in exhibiting magnitudes of sensible objects (imagination can exhibit a numerical *progression* to infinity). This subjective purposiveness is universally communicable for any being with a similarly constituted mind.

When we judge the sublime *mathematically*, the tension arises as a result of the mind's inability to comprehend reason's idea of an absolute whole in a single intuition. This problem is one of magnitude in terms of measure and falls into mathematical antinomies. When we judge the sublime *dynamically*, the problem is one of magnitude in terms of *force* and falls into dynamical antinomies. The tension is between fear and the realization that we are not really in any danger. When in an aesthetic judgement we consider nature as a might that has no power over us we say it is dynamically sublime.

Nature is regarded as dynamically sublime for aesthetic judgement only in so far as we consider it an object of fear. However, we can consider an object fearful without being afraid of it. Krishnachandra Bhattacharyya, in his essay, *The Concept of Rasa*, writes that a tragedy may be heart-rending without rendering our hearts. An object is an object of fear if we find that our ability to resist its might is insufficient. But if we judge the object in such a way that we merely *think* of the *possibility* of resisting its might, at the same time realizing that such resistance would be utterly futile, we consider the object fearful without being afraid of it. We cannot pass judgement on the sublime in nature if we are afraid. It is impossible to enjoy terror if we take it seriously, just as we cannot pass judgement on the beautiful when we have an interest in the object's existence.

Our ability to resist the might of nature is completely inadequate, yet the sight of nature's power attracts us all the more when it is most powerful. We call such objects of nature sublime because they allow us to discover in ourselves an ability to resist which gives us courage to believe we could be a match for nature's apparent omnipotence. We find our ability to judge ourselves independent of nature, in spite of our physical impotence, and our superiority over nature. Kant has in mind that may be called *moral* self-preservation, which keeps the humanity in our person from being degraded even though as human beings we would be destroyed by nature's might. We regard as small the objects of our natural concern (things like property, health and life) and so we regard nature's power as having no dominance over us as *persons* (who are capable of choosing maxims). Nature here is called sublime because it *elevates* our imagination, making it exhibit those cases where the mind can come to feel its own sublimity. We realize that we do *not* have to bow to nature when our highest principles are at stake. In the second *Critique* Kant says that through contemplating our duty to the moral law we realize that human nature can elevate itself above everything that nature can present as an incentive.

11

Conclusion

THE sublime, for Kant, is at the leading edge of the critical problem. It is defined with concern about the limits of knowledge, and with what lies beyond those limits. This may be regarded as a solution to the problem of a *deus absconditus* in the Western tradition.

Kant tells us that the final end of all knowledge is to know oneself as noumenon. While one can rationally argue for freedom from the categorical imperative, it is quite a different thing to be able to actually *experience* the supersensible, and perhaps in the end such an experience is necessary if an individually existent human being is to offer his or her inclinations in favour of the objective principle of morality. Herein lies the significance of the sublime in Kant's moral metaphysics. Through it one feels the noumenal world and may be subjectively motivated in favour of what is objectively conceived. Paton has suggested, and very much truly, that the problem of moral motivation is one of bringing reason's ideas of a moral law to an intuition and then a feeling.

The noumenon is supersensible, and so is freedom. In speaking of nature and freedom does Kant speak of two ontologically distinct worlds? He often uses language, as in the Canon of Pure Reason at the end of the first *Critique*, that might mislead. Kant does not hold that there are two ontologically distinct worlds. There is one reality which is noumenally grounded but only phenomenally known by us. We know one real world as it appears to us, although we can *conceive* this one world both as it appears to our sense experience, and as it is in itself. Hence the supersensible is not the supernatural, what is *saṁsāra* from one point of view is *nirvāna* from another. The limit and the awareness of the limit tells the entire story about the critical endeavour. Kant always meant to describe one reality approached from two different points of view. Our experience of the sublime reveals how all discourse is limited yet we still have a sense of meaningfulness lying beyond the limits of whatever discourse we can find. The experience of the sublime may reveal the limits of the senses, imagination, and understanding. This deconstructionist interpretation has its own viability as a price of metaphysical insight. And this only augments the moral interpretation of the sublime in the context of moral motivation.

Formulations of the sublime are found in the *Groundwork* and the second *Critique*. Even the term "sublime" is used adjectivally in these works, yet the point that is indicated is the link between the sublime and morality. Sublime at this point is used as a predicate ascribed to wills determined by the moral laws or, in other words, wills that have transcended determination by any natural impulse. Moral consciousness is sublime because it manifests the ultimate authority and transcendence of our rational over our sensible being. Moral consciousness arises *from* our self-transcendence towards the universal. Moreover, moral consciousness of the sublime embodies a kind of feeling, namely respect. If the sublime is understood in connection of our self-transcendent moral consciousness and feeling of respect, then it is ultimately for Kant a doorway to the supersensible. This is morally significant in that it helps to solve the problem of motivating the subject towards an objectively conceived goal.

In the context of the Introduction to the *Critique of Judgement*, the taste serves to bridge the gulf between nature and freedom. *Logically* taste may be independent of morality, this is a part of the meaning of disinterestedness or reflective aesthetic judgement of taste. But *metaphysically* taste serves morality. The *a priori* principle of reflective judgement is a mainfestation of our super-sensible being. Both theoretical and moral principles are manifestations of the supersensible. Such an interpretation could be put forward, even when Kant uses the term "supersensible" to refer to the unity which links the theoretical and moral domains together. However, it remains arguable that the sublime is construed as being occasioned by powers which transcend the self in some specifiable way. Kant's use of examples in which virtue transcends personal inclination provides an important clue as to the nature of this transcendence. And it is the grounding sublime in such self-transcendence from the sensuous level of our being to the universal that Kant arrives at, the basis of his moral theory.

Is beauty not enough? Why should Kant bring in the sublime apart from beauty? There have been challenges with regard to the place of beauty as the only or most important aesthetic quality. The sublime as a quality is to be contrasted with beauty in several ways. Ideas of pain and danger, etc., are not easily encapsulated by beauty. Burke held that beauty and sublimity are alternative qualities. Or is it as a matter of existential crises within aesthetic experience that the sublime is demanded by the aesthetic consciousness? For example, W.B. Yeats had to coin the telling expression "terrible beauty."

Kant is certainly the first of the moderns to attempt a precise definition of the sublime. The sublime, for Kant, is a unity directly antithetical to beauty. These two constitute the whole domain of aesthetic judgement. The point about the sublime is a disclosure of an experience that would remind us of our invincible freedom as moral beings, and this is intended to conquer a whole new world for aesthetic satisfaction.

Be it the beautiful or the sublime, the key to the compression of the aesthetic experience lies with Kant's usage of the term "idea." The imagination generates ideas no less a manner that reason, and in each case the ideas are either too small or too large for the concepts of the understanding. But there is a difference between the experiences of the beautiful and that of the sublime. In the case of experiencing the beautiful our cognitive faculties are at free play. The judgement of taste is both an aesthetic judgement and a judgement of the understanding in combination. There obtains the freedom of play between imagination and the law-abiding character of the understanding. The apprehension of the form delights us in a free manner. The feeling that the mind feels in its freedom, and this freedom in the play of images involves sensibility. The mind feels its freedom through sensibility. The implication of the account is that taste relates the supersensible world of freedom and the empirical world of sensation through a feeling.

The sublime, on the other hand, is presented as awe-inspiring magnitude, it invites, defers and astonishes. The sublime is a feeling and not an object of taste, only the beautiful belongs to taste. While both the beautiful and the sublime are aesthetic judgements, the idea of sublime is *contrary* to taste. However, Kant tells us that the idea of the sublime can and should be beautiful. Or else how could there be the exquisitely great poetry of the *Nāsadiya Sukta* or the apocalypse of *viśvarūpa darśana* in the *Bhagavad-Gītā?* The existence of *bibhatsa* as a *rasa* does and must abide by the canons of beauty (*camatkāra*) of literature.

The sublime inclines toward ideas of reason and hence both imagination and the understanding fail to engage it, as the form itself gets dissolved under pressure of immensity and magnitude of the presentation. The cognitive powers are rendered inadequate for it, and we are prepared for esteeming the sublime even against our sensible interest. We cannot cognize this idea of the supersensible, but it is this idea that is aroused in us when our aesthetic judging strains the imagination to its limit. The tension between imagination and reason that constitutes the sublime is the result of reason exerting a dominance via its ideas over sensibility *for the sake of* expanding sensibility commensurably with reason's own practical, i.e., moral, domain. Reason through presentation of its ideas expands and elevates sensibility by asking it to look out towards the infinite, which for sensibility can only be an abyss. Thus the experience of the sublime is possible for the fact that the imagination realizes its inadequacy in receiving ideas of reason. The experience is form of a cognitive crisis and exerts a profound liberating influence on the individual who undergoes the experience. It is as it were an experience of a moment on the edge, an encounter with the supersensible. The feeling of respect depends on cognition, but the experience of the sublime is a more immediate doorway to the supersensible. The feeling of the sublime facilitates the subjective moral motivation. The motivation might be more efficacious than the motivation provided by cognition of the moral law, perhaps more effective in terms of subjectively motivating the individual to put aside the competing subjective motive of inclination in favour of the objectively conceived moral law. The second and third *Critiques* taken together show that Kant understands moral motivation in terms both of feeling and of the rational principles of pure practical reason.

Bibliography

Reference Work on Kant

Caygill, Howard, *A Kant Dictionary,* Blackwell, Oxford, 1995.

English Translation of Kant's Works

Kant, Immannuel, *Anthropology from a Pragmatic Point of View,* tr. Victor Lyle Dowdell, South Illinois University Press, 1978. *The Critique of Judgement,* tr. Werner S. Pluhar, Indianapolis : Hackett Publishing Company, 1987.

Critique of Judgement, tr. J.H. Bernard, Hafner Publishing Co., New York and London, 1968.

The Critique of Pure Reason, tr. Norman Kemp Smith, Macmillan, London, 1929.

Immannuel Kant's The Critique of Pure Reason, tr. Norman Kemp Smith, Macmillan, London, 1961.

Lectures on Ethics, tr. Louis Infield, Introduction by Lewis White Beck, Methuen, London, 1979.

Lectures on Metaphysics, tr. and ed. Karl Ameriks and Steve Naragon, The Cambridge Edition of the Works of Immannuel Kant, Cambridge University Press, 1997.

Observations on the Feeling of the Beautiful and the Sublime, tr. John T. Goldthwait, Berkeley; University of California Press, 1960.

Critique of Practical Reason, tr. Lewis White Beck, Bobbs-Merrill, New York, 1959.

Foundations of the Metaphysics of Morals, tr. Lewis White Beck, Bobbs-Merrill, New York, 1959.

First Introduction to the Critique of Judgement, tr. James Haden, Bobbs-Merrill, New York, 1965.

Other Works

A Treatise of Human Nature, ed., L.A. Selby-Bigge, Oxford, Oxford University Press, 1964 reprint.

Allison, Henry, *Kant's Theory of Freedom,* Cambridge University Press, Cambridge, 1990.

Beck, Lewis White, *A Commentary on Kant's Critique of Practical Reason,* Chicago, The University of Chicago Press, 1960.

Bernstein, John Andrew, *Shaftesbury Rousseau, and Kant : An Introduction to the Conflict between Aesthetic and Moral Values in Modern Thought,* London and Toronto : Associated Universtiy Press, 1980.

Burke, Edmund, *On the Sublime and the Beautiful,* ed., C.W. Elliot, P.F. Collier and Son Corporation, New York, 1937.

Cohen Ted, "Why Beauty is a Symbol of Morality," in *Essays in Kant Aesthetics,* ed. Ted Cohen and Paul Guyer, Chicago: The University of Chicago Press.

Crowther, Paul, *The Kantian Sublime : From Morality to Art,* Oxford University Press, 1989.

Guyer Paul, *Kant and the Claims of Taste,* Cambridge, Harvard University Press, 1979.

Hume, David, *Essays Moral, Political and Literary,* ed., E.F. Miller, Indianapolis, Liberty Classics, 1985.

Kant and the Experience of Freedom : Essays on Aesthetics and Morality, Cambridge, Cambridge University Press, 1993.

Kant's Aesthetic Theory : An Introduction, New York : St. Martin's Press, 1979.

Kemal Salim, *Kant and Fine Art: An Essay on Kant and the Philosophy of Fine Art and Culture*, Oxford, Oxford University Press, 1986.

Makkreel, Rudolf A., *Imagination and Interpretation in Kant : The Hermeneutical Import of the Critique of Judgment*, Chicago, University of Chicago Press, 1990.

Paton, H.J. *The Categorical Imperative : A Study in Kant's Moral Philosophy*, The University of Chicago Press, 1948.

Schaper, Eva, *Studies in Kant's Aesthetics*, Edinburgh University Press, 1979.

Zammito, John H., *The Genesis of Kant's Critique of Judgment*, Chicago, The University of Chicago Press, 1992.

Zimmerman, Robert L., "Kant: The Aesthetic Judgment" in *Kant : A Collection of Critical Essays*, ed. Robert Raul Wolff, Modern Studies in Philosophy Series, Notre Dame: University of Notre Dame Press, 1967.

Miscellaneous

Aurobindo Sri, *The Future Poetry*, Sri Aurobindo Ashram, Pondicherry, 1985.

Bhattacharyya, Krishnachandra, *Studies in Philosophy*, vol. 1, Calcutta, 1960.

Goethe, *Faust*, Part One, tr. Philip Wayne, Penguin Books, 1963.

MacNeice, Louis, *Selected Poems*, Penguin Books, 1964.

Tagore, Rabindranath, *Collected Poems and Plays*, Macmillan, London, 1961.

Yeats, W.B., *Selected Poetry*, Rupa, Calcutta, 1992.

Index